The Spanish Missions
of San Antonio

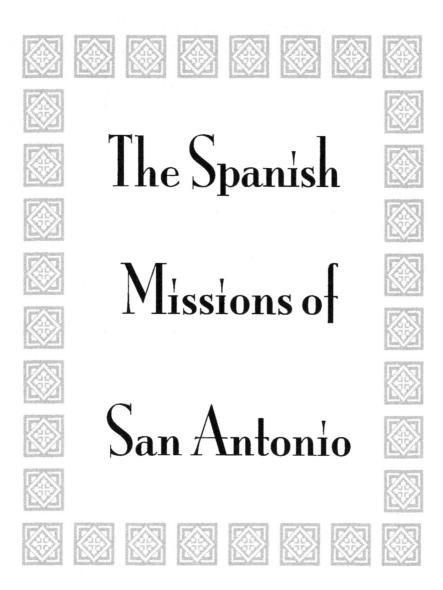

The Spanish Missions of San Antonio

Lewis F. Fisher

MAVERICK BOOKS / TRINITY UNIVERSITY PRESS
San Antonio

Published by Maverick Books, an imprint of Trinity University Press
San Antonio, Texas 78212

Cover design by Robert Vito Salinas, DVS Design
Author photo by Mary M. Fisher
Cover images: iStock/1093752532/scgerding, iStock/509210141/Dean_Fikar, iStock/178731007/Dean_Fikar, iStock/546200514/Sean Pavone Photo

Half title page: Restoration of frescoes at Mission Concepción's convento library ceiling revealed a mestizo face—emanating sunlike rays—thought to represent the face of God. Painted by Indian artists, it mixes Christian and Indian motifs and bears similarities to designs in some churches of the era in central Mexico.

Frontispiece: Across the convent courtyard at Mission San José is an open door to the adjoining church's sacristy, completed in 1777, five years before the church.

978-1-59534-713-8 paper

Trinity University Press strives to produce its books using methods and materials in an environmentally sensitive manner. We favor working with manufacturers that practice sustainable management of all natural resources, produce paper using recycled stock, and manage forests with the best possible practices for people, biodiversity, and sustainability. The press is a member of the Green Press Initiative, a nonprofit program dedicated to supporting publishers in their efforts to reduce their impacts on endangered forests, climate change, and forest-dependent communities.

CIP data on file at the Library of Congress

27 26 25 24 23 | 8 7 6 5 4

Contents

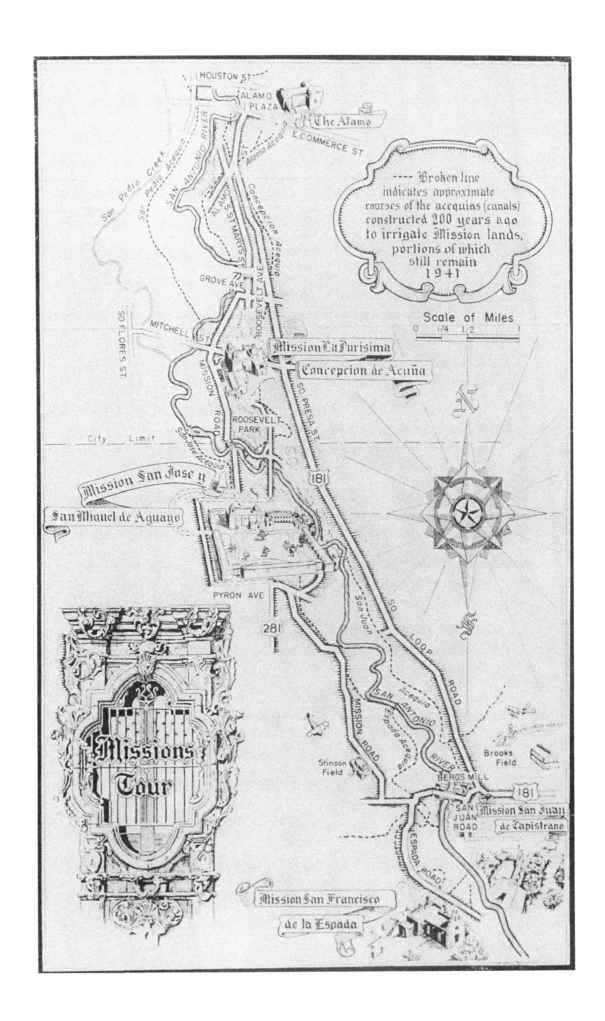

Introduction

Dotting the winding banks of the San Antonio River for eight miles below its headwaters are the remains of five Spanish missions. Once links in a loose chain of settlement across the northern reaches of New Spain from Florida to California, they form the largest cluster of Spanish missions in the United States.

Some mission buildings are majestic in their settings, with delicate baroque carvings in native limestone and still-bright frescoes, one daring to portray the face of God. Others are more rough-hewn testimonies to the faith which built the missions and sustained them on a vast and hostile frontier.

The first, Mission San Antonio de Valero, was established in 1718, giving birth to what became the city of San Antonio. More than a century later, priests and Indian converts long departed, its embattled ruins achieved immortality as the Alamo.

The second, San José y San Miguel de Aguayo, "Queen of the Missions of New Spain," founded two years later, was the most successful Spanish mission in Texas. San José's baroque sacristy window is considered by many to be the finest example of Spanish colonial sculpture in Spanish North America.

The three other missions moved in 1731 from the troubled Spanish East Texas frontier with French Louisiana to the relative safety of San Antonio—Nuestra Señora de la Purísima Concepción de Acuña, San Juan Capistrano and San Francisco de la Espada. Concepción's twin-towered church remains the nation's best-preserved Spanish colonial structure. Three-belled *espadañas* are distinctive signatures of San Juan and of Espada, whose stone aqueduct is the nation's oldest in continuous use.

By 1824, all five missions had been closed and their churches turned over to local Catholic authorities, with other buildings and lands divided among remaining mission Indians or sold.

But even in decay the missions held a special appeal. Decades of efforts to preserve and restore them climaxed in 1978 with creation of San Antonio Missions National Historical Park, preserving the four southern missions. Sanctuaries at each now serve independent parishes. In the heart of downtown the fifth—the Alamo—is owned by the State of Texas and administered by the Daughters of the Republic of Texas as a shrine to Texas liberty.

Each mission has its own tale of survival, achievement, decline and, finally, rescue and restoration, reflecting unique tumults and triumphs over the course of nearly three centuries.

The image of a cross was included during casting of the bell for Mission Concepción's church, dedicated in 1755.

Facing page: Restoration of Mission San José and its opening as a state park in 1941 brought increased tourist interest in all five missions. This Work Projects Administration guidebook map shows the missions' physical relationship to each other, to downtown San Antonio and to the San Antonio River.

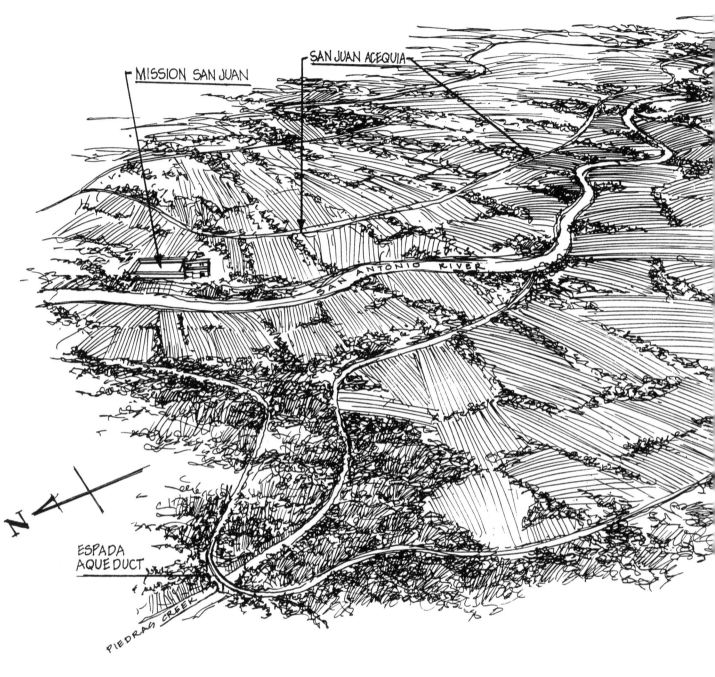

MISSION SAN JUAN

SAN JUAN ACEQUIA

SAN ANTONIO RIVER

N

ESPADA
AQUEDUCT

PIEDRAS CREEK

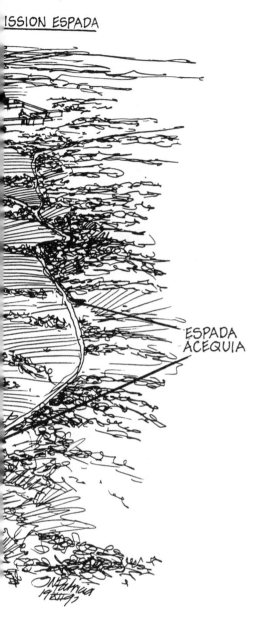

MISSION ESPADA

ESPADA
ACEQUIA

Next to building a church, an irrigation system was a missionary's top priority. Using techniques from Moslem Spain, acequias were dug following contours of the land. Those of missions San Juan and Espada, sketched above looking down-stream to the southeast, stretched several miles before returning to the river. A wing-shaped diversion dam of stone and brush, lower left on opposite page, raised the river to flow into Espada's still-functioning system, begun in 1731. It spans a creek with a double-arched stone aqueduct, lower right.

Apostólico de Santa Cruz de Querétaro, founded in 1683, and the Colegio de Nuestra Señora de Guadalupe de Zacatecas, founded in 1707. There missionaries were trained for the field, architects drew plans for mission churches and logistics were coordinated.

Using grants of land and materials provided by the crown, South Texas missions were established on well-drained farming sites with access to water. For irrigation, each mission had its own system of *acequias*, or irrigation ditches, a term derived from the Arabic word *al-sáquiyá*. Dug by resident mission Indians, acequias used irrigation principles that originated in ancient Mesopotamia and were perfected in Moorish Spain. A diversion dam raised the river level so water could flow into a ditch engineered, sometimes with the aid of aqueducts, with a slight downhill grade. Channels could extend for several miles before returning to the river.

Temporary buildings of grass and straw or of vertical posts chinked with mud—*jacales*—housed the one or two missionaries and their potential converts. Permanent buildings utilized local limestone, which was cut with relative ease but hardened when exposed to the elements. Construction was often supervised by Tlaxcaltecan Indians from central Mexico who for generations served as builders for the Aztecs. Accustomed to primitive work-ing conditions and instructed in Spanish design by builders from Spain, they also trained local Indians in construction techniques.

Outside perimeter walls protecting the compound from hostile Indians were acequia-irrigated *huertas*—orchards and small gar-dens—and, beyond, *labores*, larger fields for such crops as corn, beans, squash, cotton and sugarcane. Farther away were mission ranches, which adapted Mexican livestock-raising techniques and contributed to development of the western cattle industry. Indian cowboys—*vaqueros*—cared for the livestock that produced beef as well as wool for mission looms. Surplus crops and livestock could be sold or bartered to other missions or to townspeople.

The process of transforming nomadic tribes into settled farm-ers and Spanish citizens was supposed to take ten years. After that the missions were to be secularized. Their churches were to be turned into parish churches, run not by missionaries of an inde-pendent order but by parish priests, and their lands were to be divided among the new citizen farmers or sold at auction.

Establishing the San Antonio Missions

Indians in Florida and New Mexico were accustomed to living in towns, making it easier for them to adapt to an ongoing life—in one place—ordered by the sound of a mission bell.

Inhabiting inland Texas, however, were more than 150 small tribes of hunter-gatherers known collectively as Coahuiltecans. They migrated each season to the nearest food source, living on a diet of berries, fruits, nuts and seeds plus birds, game and fish. They dressed in animal hides, painted and tattooed their bodies and worshiped spirits in rituals led by medicine men—*shamans*.

FACING PAGE, ABOVE: STEVEN N. PATRICIA, CONCEPT ARTWORK–DEPARTMENT OF INTERIOR, NATIONAL PARK SERVICE; LEFT, THE INSTITUTE OF TEXAN CULTURES; RIGHT, SAN ANTONIO CONSERVATION SOCIETY

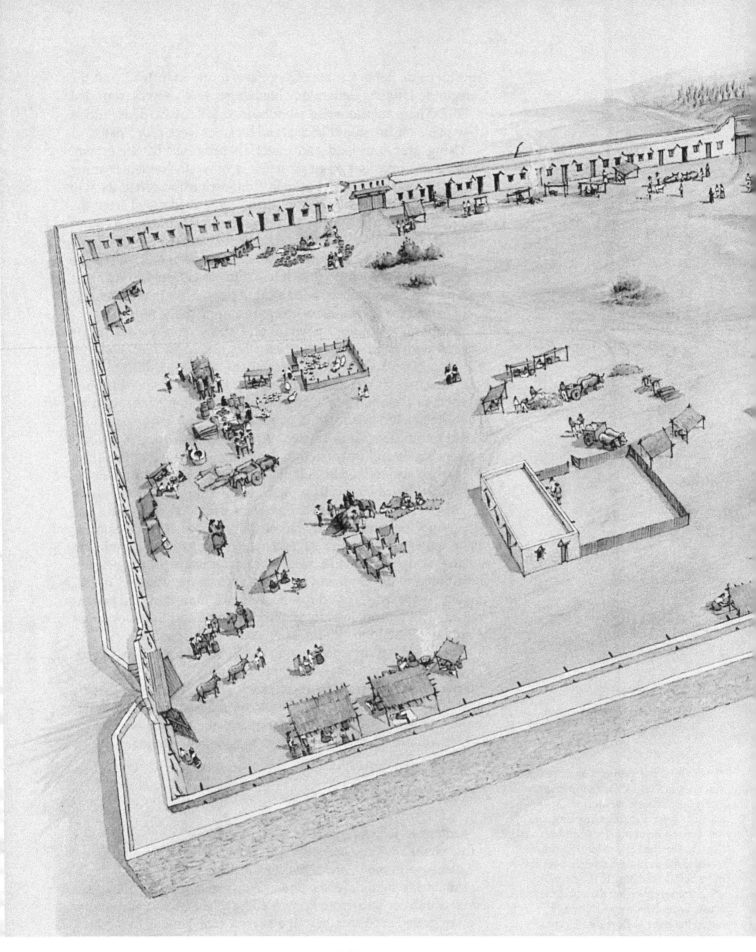

San Antonio's Mission San José, the most successful Spanish mission in Texas, is having a busy morning about 1780. Near the Indian barracks at top left, kilns are firing pottery at a workshop, as, below, goods are unloaded and inspected, and hides from the mission ranch's cattle are sorted and

sold to visiting Spaniards. Near the vaulted-roof granary at the compound's opposite corner,
workers on scaffolds finishing the church paint designs on its tower. Dyed textiles dry on
racks to the left of the garden outside the convento, the rear wall of which is under repair.

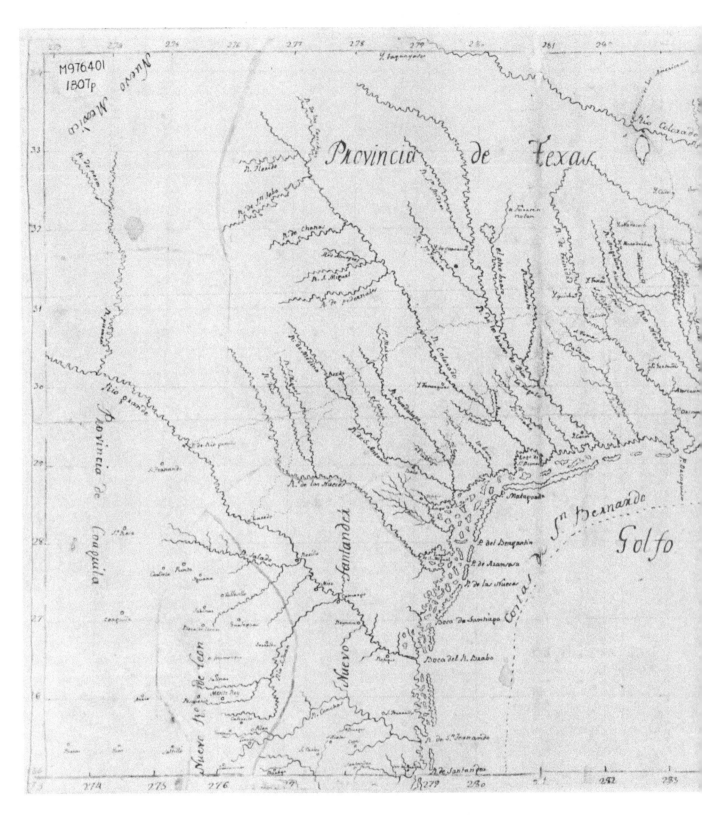

M976401
1807p

Provincia de Texas

Provincia de Coahuila

Nuevo Reyno de Leon

Nuevo Santander

S.ⁿ Bernardo

Golfo

Rivers loomed large for missionaries journeying from Mexico to the East Texas frontier with French Louisiana. In this Spanish map of 1807, the Nueces separates the provinces of Texas and Nuevo Santander. "Bexar"—San Antonio—can be spotted at the head of the "R. de S. Antonio" north of the Nueces.

Changing virtually every pattern of this life within a relatively short time presented Franciscans with an enormous challenge.

The first Spanish missions within present-day Texas were established in 1682 in the region of El Paso, then part of the province of New Mexico. Within the borders of Spanish Texas, the first missions began in 1690, with the founding of two in East Texas by Franciscans from the college at Querétaro. They ran into difficulty

THE INSTITUTE OF TEXAN CULTURES

immediately. For the French on the Louisiana frontier were close to their supply base downriver in New Orleans, and had already built strong alliances among East Texas Indians.

The Spanish in East Texas were also handicapped not only by the distance from their nearest mission stronghold, 400 miles to the southwest near the Rio Grande at present-day Guerrero in Mexico, but by the region's topography. The harsh overland journey was made even more tortuous by rivers that ran in the wrong direction—northwest to southeast—and could not be crossed after heavy rains.

On top of all this, an epidemic that took the lives of 3,000 Indians was blamed on the Spaniards, and the Indians threatened a massacre. In 1693 the two missions were abandoned.

Trying again, in 1716 the Querétarans and Zacatecans each established three missions in Spanish East Texas, protected this time by presidios garrisoned by Spanish soldiers. The presidio at Los Adaes, close to the west bank of the Red River near present-day Robeline, Louisiana, was made the capital of Spanish Texas.

Strategists seeking a way station to support these missions had to look no farther than the lush headwaters of a river a third of the way from their supply base on the Rio Grande. The place had been discovered by an expedition to the first East Texas missions in 1691 and was named for St. Anthony of Padua. A Franciscan missionary from Querétaro, Father Antonio de San Buenaventura y Olivares, was among those who visited the site in 1709. He thought it an ideal location for a mission.

On May 1, 1718 Father Olivares established a mission he named San Antonio de Valero near the springs of San Pedro Creek, two miles west of the headwaters of the San Antonio River. Four days later soldiers set up a presidio nearby.

The next year the French invaded East Texas. Missionaries and some loyal Indians fell back to San Antonio. They did not return for two years. Father Antonio Margil de Jesús, a veteran missionary from Zacatecas who had helped set up missions in East Texas, quickly saw an opportunity for a new mission on the San Antonio River. He proposed a Zacatecan mission to proselytize the territory south of San Antonio while the Querétarans' Mission San Antonio de Valero served the land to the north, the manner in which the two colleges divided their work in East Texas.

His proposal accepted, Father Margil walked to San Antonio in the Franciscan way of traveling on foot. In 1720 he established Mission San José y San Miguel de Aguayo on the San Antonio River, four miles south of Mission San Antonio de Valero. Between the two, Querétarans in 1722 set up Mission San Francisco Xavier de Nájera, though it soon merged with San Antonio de Valero.

Then, as part of a short-lived agreement with France, an East Texas presidio was closed to realign the frontier. The three nearby Querétaran missions, now without military protection, abandoned East Texas in 1730. Missionaries and some mission Indians hauled goods and supplies by wagon as they drove their livestock west, stopping first at sites on the Colorado River at present-day

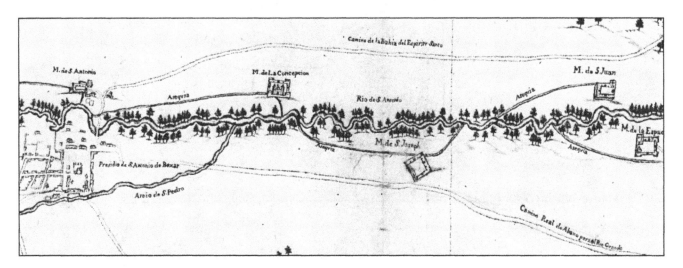

Mission San Antonio de Valero and a military presidio to protect it were established in 1718. By the time this map—looking east—was drawn in 1764, the presidio and villa of San Fernando de Béxar were on the west bank of the river, shown at far left, and Mission San Antonio de Valero was on the opposite side of the river's Great Bend. Four newer missions were on alternate sides of the river downstream.

Austin. They received permission to move to the banks of the upper San Antonio River in 1731 from the head of the Querétaran college, Father Isidro Félix de Espinosa, who had helped Father Olivares scout the site of San Antonio in 1709.

The transplanted missions took the names Nuestra Señora de la Purísima Concepción de Acuña, San Juan Capistrano and San Franciso de la Espada. The four missions downstream from San Antonio de Valero were on alternate sides of the river—Concepción on the east, San José on the west, San Juan Capistrano on the east and, finally, Espada on the west. In two expeditions through the surrounding countryside Spaniards gathered nearly 1,000 Indians for the new missions.

The three missions were set up within days of the arrival of San Antonio's only large group of colonial immigrants, 55 Spaniards from the Canary Islands. The stage was set for decades of quarreling among civilians, soldiers and missionaries over the region's land, water, livestock and proposed use of Indian labor.

The worst problems, however, came from the outside, as Texas Indian tribes endured an upheaval intensified by their enemies' new mobility on Spanish horses. The small tribes were being squeezed from the north by their traditional foes, the Apaches, who were being pushed by Comanches migrating from the plains. To the east were the Wichita, armed by the French. And moving up from the south were the Spanish.

The missions offered the less aggressive tribes a safe haven.

Mission Life

The task of attracting Indians into the missions began with symbolic communication, by intriguing them with elaborate vestments, statues and rituals. The ice broken, Indians were lured inside with gifts of bells, beads and clothing.

Each mission housed Indians from different tribes. This caused a communications problem, since many different Indian dialects were spoken. A priest at Mission Concepción sought to make the

Facing page: The restored chapel of Mission San Juan, like the three other church buildings in San Antonio Missions National Historical Park, serves as a parish church in a unique arrangement with the National Park Service.

In the missions, Indian families were taught to live like Europeans. This cutaway view shows San José's Indian quarters, built inside perimeter walls that protected against hostile tribes like that of the Comanche chieftain below.

Palajats' tribal tongue the common language for his converts. But the most workable solution seemed to be attempting to teach the Indians Spanish.

The next step was Christian conversion, followed by spiritual growth honed by the disciplines of mission life.

Indian novices woke to their new world at sunrise, as bells called them to Mass and to religious instruction. After a corn dish for breakfast, the day's work began, whether in fields or in mission workshops. Mission bells at noon rang the call to hearty meals of corn, vegetables, fruit and, on Sundays, beef from cattle raised on mission ranches. A siesta followed, then the afternoon's work. Ringing of the evening Angelus brought the Indians back for religious services and the day's last meal, usually more corn, beans and fish.

To teach the principles of governing, each mission was organized in the style of the villages of central Mexico. Mission Indians likewise elected leaders to govern their own *pueblo* within the framework of basic decisions made by a Spaniard—in the case of the missions, the priest.

Franciscans quickly found that giving instructions was easier than getting them carried out. Whatever the task, some found the Indians "so slow and careless, it is always necessary for a Spaniard to watch over them." Nor was spiritual redirection easy. Indians "are more concerned about having food in abundance than with any fear of life eternal," grumbled one missionary.

TOP: STEVEN N. PATRICIA, ARTWORK–DEPARTMENT OF INTERIOR, NATIONAL PARK SERVICE; BELOW: LARGE DETAIL
FROM PAINTING BY THEODORE GENTILZ, COURTESY OF THE WITTE MUSEUM, SAN ANTONIO, TEXAS

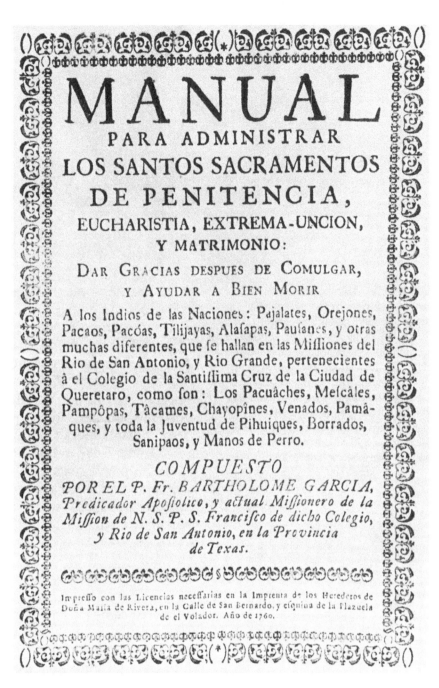

MANUAL
PARA ADMINISTRAR
LOS SANTOS SACRAMENTOS
DE PENITENCIA,
EUCHARISTIA, EXTREMA-UNCION,
Y MATRIMONIO:
DAR GRACIAS DESPUES DE COMULGAR,
Y AYUDAR A BIEN MORIR

A los Indios de las Naciones: Pajalates, Orejones,
Pacaos, Pacóas, Tilijayas, Alasapas, Pausanes, y otras
muchas diferentes, que se hallan en las Missiones del
Rio de San Antonio, y Rio Grande, pertenecientes
à el Colegio de la Santissima Cruz de la Ciudad de
Queretaro, como son: Los Pacuàches, Mescàles,
Pampópas, Tàcames, Chayopînes, Venados, Pamà-
ques, y toda la Juventud de Pihuiques, Borrados,
Sanipaos, y Manos de Perro.

COMPUESTO
POR EL P. Fr. BARTHOLOME GARCIA,
Predicador Apostolico, y actual Missionero de la
Mission de N. S. P. S. Francisco de dicho Colegio,
y Rio de San Antonio, en la Provincia
de Texas.

Impresso con las Licencias necessarias en la Imprenta de los Herederos de
Doña Maria de Rivera, en la Calle de San Bernardo, y esquina de la Plazuela
de el Volador. Año de 1760.

Confounded, as were other missionaries, by the dialects of the numerous Texas Indian tribes, Father Bartholomé García studied Coahuiltecan tongues while he was an assistant to the missionary at San Antonio's Mission Espada. In 1760 his work was published in Mexico as a manual for missionaries wishing to conduct sacraments in the Indians' native tongues. It has been termed the first textbook of Texas.

Indians suffered from a high infant mortality rate and fell easy prey to European diseases, most disastrously in San Antonio to an epidemic of smallpox and measles in 1739. Moreover, their health in general was poor, aggravated, no doubt, by the psychological stress of adapting to a radically new lifestyle.

Desertions were common. "It is rare if they do not flee . . . two or three times, sometimes going as far as 100 leagues away," a friar complained, for nomadic Indians felt a natural impulse to suddenly wander off and had trouble understanding that in the eyes of the Spaniards joining a mission was a binding contract, and that breaking it would inevitably result in punishment.

Sometimes Indians went no farther than the next mission. In the mid-1730s, a group of Tacame Indians left Mission San José and joined Espada, only to desert when not given permission to

Although San Antonio's missions had passed their peak by the end of the eighteenth century, some progress continued. In the 1790s a small flour mill was built into a slope beside the acequia along San José's northern wall. The slow-flowing water gained force when the gate, shown alongside the acequia at the right of the mill, was opened and water entered a chute and dropped onto the millwheel in a subterranean room, turning a grindstone before flowing out.

move to San Antonio de Valero. Missionaries from San José made several trips to gather 77 of the Tecames and escort them, after all, to San Antonio de Valero.

Hostile Apaches and Comanches were a strong incentive to keep errant Indians within mission walls. Far-flung mission ranches were particularly vulnerable to Indian attacks, though even civilians, inexperienced at farming and ranching, sometimes raided mission herds themselves.

As Indian attacks abated, San Antonio's five mission ranches in 1762 had 5,487 cattle, 560 saddle horses, 1,280 mares and 15,200 sheep and goats, plus donkeys and mules. By this time the total number of Indians at San Antonio's five missions had leveled off at around 1,000—about twice the civilian population of the town of San Antonio, largest in Spanish Texas.

Decline and Disarray

In 1763 came the end of the French and Indian War—fought in Europe as the Seven Years' War—and Louisiana was transferred from France to Spain. Texas was no longer a frontier province but an interior province. Hard-to-reach Los Adaes lost its strategic importance, and in 1773 the capital was moved to San Antonio.

San Antonio's Spanish missions also lost their strategic importance as bastions against French expansion just as Russian designs on the Pacific coast were giving the present-day state of California new strategic significance for New Spain. Extending the mission system seemed a natural development for the west coast.

Franciscans began building the latter-day missions of California in 1769 using techniques perfected in Texas. They benefited from California having the highest Indian population density in North America, making it easier for priests to replace Indians dying of disease in the California missions than it was in the more sparsely populated reaches of Texas.

Soon the Franciscan college in Querétaro was tapped to staff the southern Arizona and northern Mexico missions of the Jesuits, expelled from the Spanish empire in 1767. Querétaran missionar-

Ranches of Spanish missions in Texas contributed to development of the western cattle industry. This brand was used for cattle on Mission Espada's ranch, its headquarters ruins now owned by the National Park Service.

ABOVE: DRAWING BY ERNST SCHUCHARD, DRT LIBRARY AT THE ALAMO; BELOW: SAN ANTONIO MISSIONS NATIONAL HISTORICAL PARK

ies left Texas for the former Jesuit missions in 1772, turning over their four San Antonio missions to their Zacatecan brothers.

By now the Franciscans were thinking that the time to close the Texas missions outright was at hand. Most of the remaining Indians in the region had been absorbed into the Spanish culture, often intermarrying with Spaniards, speaking their language and professing their faith.

By 1793 the three dozen missions established at one time or another in Spanish Texas had shrunk to eight. Five were in San Antonio, where San José held the local record for Indian baptisms—2,000 over the course of a century. The others were in Karankawa territory to the southeast near present-day Goliad—Nuestra Señora del Espíritu Santo de Zúñiga and Nuestra Señora del Rosario, not far from the new Nuestra Señora del Refugio, the last Spanish mission founded in Texas.

"Everything, everything is turned around," lamented one missionary. "There are few Indians and many hired hands. There are few cattle, and even so, no one to sell them to because there are too many grazers. Even if the missions had an abundance of corn there are too many farmers, so many that some have abandoned agriculture."

So the missions were secularized as they were to have been long before, had the wandering natives become settled, Christianized farmers on the Texas frontier, as intended, within ten years. Mission San Antonio de Valero, increasingly part of the life of San Antonio just across the river, was completely closed in 1793. The next year the process began gradually at the other four.

The government of the Republic of Mexico completed the transition. On February 29, 1824, Father José Antonio Díaz de León, the last Franciscan missionary in Texas, turned over San Antonio's four remaining mission churches and chapels to the San Fernando parish representative of the Bishop of Monterrey, overseer of Catholic churches in Texas.

Though San Antonio's missions ceased functioning as such by 1824, and their lands were dispersed, their churches and chapels remained under Catholic ownership—not of an independent missionary order but of the local diocese.

The structures were assigned to the priest at San Antonio's parish church of San Fernando, right, completed in 1758 on Plaza de las Islas, or Main Plaza.

First Mission South View

A half-century after they were closed, San Antonio's missions were in varying stages of disrepair, the southern ones identified no longer by name but by number in order of their distance from town. Concepción's church remained intact, although what was left of its adjoining convento had become the home of chickens and other farm animals.

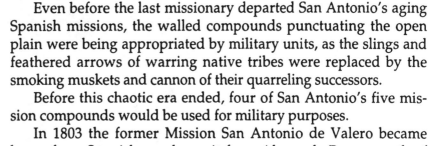

2. The Missions' Rescue and Restoration

Future bishop Jean Marie Odin in 1841 got the Republic of Texas to confirm Catholic Church ownership of the former Spanish mission churches.

Even before the last missionary departed San Antonio's aging Spanish missions, the walled compounds punctuating the open plain were being appropriated by military units, as the slings and feathered arrows of warring native tribes were replaced by the smoking muskets and cannon of their quarreling successors.

Before this chaotic era ended, four of San Antonio's five mission compounds would be used for military purposes.

In 1803 the former Mission San Antonio de Valero became home for a Spanish cavalry unit from Alamo de Parras south of the Rio Grande, giving the old mission a nickname passed into history when it became the site of the massacre of the Texas garrison in 1836. Once the Republic of Texas was annexed by the United States in 1845, the U.S. Army refurbished what was left and used the Alamo as a supply depot for more than three decades.

The lands of Mission Concepción, occupied by Mexican revolutionary forces in 1813, were the site of a Texas Revolutionary War victory in 1835. During the Mexican War, Concepción's church was used as a U.S. Army supply depot, as was the church of Mission San José.

Having driven off pickets of the Mexican Army that had fortified Mission Espada, Texas soldiers in 1835 moved into the Espada compound several weeks before retaking San Antonio from a Mexican force.

A turning point in the fortunes of the former missions came in 1840, when future bishop Jean Marie Odin was named to revive the Catholic Church in the Republic of Texas. The next year the Congress of the Republic of Texas confirmed the church's ownership claim of mission churches and portions of adjoining plazas and fields. As bishop, Odin began to repurchase key mission land in private ownership.

Mission San Antonio de Valero was never again used for religious purposes. But during the 1850s Catholic religious orders were moved to Concepción, where mission farmlands supported a new school, and to San José, where an attempt was made to reconstruct the convento as a monastery.

Many of the missions' crumbling outbuildings and perimeter walls, however, if not turned into barns or makeshift homes, became, in effect, public rock quarries. The physical environment

Two perennial attractions of San Antonio—the missions and the river—were boosted as premier "winter resort" tourist destinations once the railroad reached San Antonio in 1877. At the lower left of the railroad's promotional brochure cover is an engraving of the surviving facade of Espada's chapel.

also changed, as overgrazing after the Civil War transformed the grassy plains of South Texas into "cactus-choked brush country."

Known by Their Numbers

In 1877 the Galveston, Harrisburg and San Antonio Railway—later part of the Southern Pacific—at last linked San Antonio with mainstream America. At once railroad promoters eager to increase passenger traffic began boosting distant San Antonio as a winter resort filled with remarkable sights.

At the top of the list were the old missions, though their original names were forgotten. San Antonio de Valero was "the

After the turn of the century, tourists arriving by rail could hire chauffeured automobiles and reach the missions easily, as did those in the top photo who made it to San José despite muddy roads. San José's granary buttresses made an uncomfortable perch for ladies with long dresses, but bustles did not hinder ladies like the one at lower right snapped entering Concepción's church by one of the first Kodak cameras, which produced circular images.

San Antonio's chapter of the Daughters of the Republic of Texas became the first group to take action to save the missions as architectural landmarks. In 1902 the ladies gathered supplies and raised funds to erect a six-foot fence around San José's church, keeping stray cows out while allowing tourists in through a gate. But by the time the visitors above arrived in their surrey in 1903, the turret enclosing the tower's stairway had collapsed in a pile of rubble, leaving a gaping doorway halfway up the tower's east wall. A brace behind the decaying facade of the roofless church, however, halted growth of the crack over the doorway which had already split the icon of Our Lady of Guadalupe.

A major example of Mission Revival architecture was San Antonio's Missouri, Kansas & Texas Railway depot. New York architect Frederick Sterner measured the facade of Mission Concepción's church to duplicate its twin towers, added an entrance reminiscent of San José's and designed roof gables typical of California.

Alamo," vacated by the Army before the State of Texas bought the church in 1883 for its battle memories—the first purchase of a landmark for historic preservation west of the Mississippi River. The other four missions were identified merely by number, in the order of their progression down the river.

The "first mission" was Concepción, its tumbledown convento sheltering wagons and farm animals.

After the Alamo, the biggest tourist draw was the still imposing though now roofless and domeless church of the second mission, San José, where souvenir hunters arriving in growing caravans of tourist carriages took an increasing toll. The massive wooden front doors disappeared, the belfry stairway collapsed, bits of ornate carving were chiseled off as souvenirs and vandals began dismembering the stone saints who guarded the portal.

The derelict chapel of the third mission, San Juan, was re-roofed by the priest who then rebuilt the chapel of the fourth mission, Espada, using it as his parish church and rebuilding its convento as his residence.

But soon public sympathy for the plight of San Antonio's missions was roused by two secular movements, both originating in California.

A new appreciation for Spanish missions in general was sparked when eastern architects in the 1880s hit upon indigenous mission architecture for projects in Florida, New Mexico and California, where Mission Revival became the rage. Within a decade both the Southern Pacific and the Atchison, Topeka and Santa Fe railroads began spreading Mission Revival from California throughout the Southwest as the style for their new stations.

Mission Revival burst into San Antonio in 1902 with the Southern Pacific's railroad station, a central element of its facade being a curved gable parapet similar to that added 50 years before to the old Alamo church. The motif spread throughout Texas as the Alamo Revival variation of Mission Revival.

After the church of Mission San Antonio de Valero was purchased by the State of Texas for its role as the Alamo, its restoration took on a life independent of the preservation of San Antonio's four other missions. Here the old church is getting a vaulted concrete roof in time for the 1936 Texas Centennial.

The approximate site of San Antonio's short-lived Mission San Francisco Xavier de Nájera was marked near Mission Concepción during the Texas Centennial.

By World War I, Mission Revival had evolved into the more ornate Spanish Colonial Revival, signature style of the 1920s construction boom in San Antonio, the largest city in the largest state.

To this style San Antonio contributed the pattern of San José's baroque sacristy window, by then recognized as perhaps the finest example of Spanish Colonial design anywhere in Spanish North America.

Following this newfound respect for Spanish America's architectural legacy came an appreciation of the surviving Spanish missions themselves. This awareness gained momentum in 1894, as several of California's crumbling missions were leased from the Catholic Church and independently restored by Charles F. Lummis's Landmarks Club of California.

Within eight years San Antonio's redoubtable pioneer preservationist Adina De Zavala set out on the same course as the leader of the Daughters of the Republic of Texas's local chapter, which she sometimes referred to as "the landmarks club of Texas."

Restoration Begins

In the spring of 1902 Miss De Zavala's organization began San Antonio's first community effort to restore the missions by raising funds and scrounging materials from local businessmen to make temporary repairs at San José. That fall the Catholic diocese gave the group a five-year lease to repair Mission San Juan under terms similar to those the Landmarks Club negotiated in California. But the "landmarks club of Texas" was soon sidetracked to the Alamo to save San Antonio de Valero's old convento.

Bishop John William Shaw in 1911 committed the Catholic diocese to restoring San Antonio's four southern mission churches, an effort carried out with some success through his chancellor, Father William Wheeler Hume. Automobiles made the missions ever more popular places of pilgrimage for travelers, including members of the Vatican Choir, who detoured from a national tour in 1919 to sing at both Concepción and San José.

Railroads aided the growth of mission neighborhoods by giving their residents easy access to the city. On its new "Mission Route" east of the river, the San Antonio and Aransas Pass Railroad in 1885 opened a station at Berg's Mill near Mission San Juan. West of the river, in 1912 the San José station opened on the new San Antonio, Uvalde and Gulf Railroad.

Preservation of some of the historic openness of part of the region was assured when the first of a major complex of cemeteries was opened in 1909 by the Mission Cemetery Company, its chapel a converted building of the beef extract company previously on the site.

Formal suburban development crept to the southern missions the next year, when the Concepción Land Company platted its Mission Park addition just east of Mission Concepción. Unplanned development had already obliterated San José's mission plaza, where small houses had popped up and roads crisscrossed the plaza, covering outlines of mission walls. By the early 1920s it was obviously a matter of time before urban sprawl would fill the open countryside surrounding San José.

While the Catholic Church focused on saving the mission churches, the concept of preserving entire mission compounds began capturing the imaginations of secular preservationists, many of them non-Catholic. One such preservationist, Rena Maverick Green, a frequent visitor to England, picked up on a tenet of Great Britain's National Trust: to preserve not just a landmark but also its context in its original natural setting.

Mrs. Green sounded the cry that San José's entire environment must be rescued, not just the church but also its outlying buildings, the walled compound and the old mission fields, preferably as part of a national park including all four southern missions.

In 1924 the new San Antonio Conservation Society, cofounded by Mrs. Green, started efforts to purchase what was left of San José's vaulted-roof granary. As the society began buying

By the 1920s commercialism spreading toward San José reached the confines of the old mission compound. When the area began to be cleared for restoration, a recalcitrant refreshment stand operator profiting from the tourist trade had to be removed, in 1932, by court order.

In the absence of effective efforts to save San Antonio's mission complexes, preserving them became the primary goal of the San Antonio Conservation Society soon after its founding in 1924. By 1935 the Conservation Society not only owned the mission granary but was directing its reconstruction, above, by federal relief workers, who also began rebuilding the walls and roof of San José's church itself (*facing page*).

back the old mission compound piecemeal, it sold one adjacent tract to the Catholic Church as a friary for the Franciscans, who returned to San Antonio in 1931 after an absence of 107 years.

With the Depression came federally subsidized workers to clear the San José compound and rebuild its perimeter walls and buildings. In 1941 the Conservation Society, the Catholic Church and Bexar County—which surrendered its roadway through the compound—gave land to create Mission San José State Park, promptly named a National Historic Site.

Creating a National Park

The goal of creating a national park proved as elusive as the Franciscans' original challenge of transforming native hunter-gatherers into European-style farmers. Restoration work progressed intermittently at all four missions. In 1967, as awareness of the potential impact of tourism grew with the approach of San Antonio's world's fair, HemisFair '68, the first bill to create a missions national park was introduced in Congress.

But negotiations and counterproposals dragged on for 11 more years, as the prospect of religious services in church-owned sanc-

FACING PAGE AND ABOVE: THE *SAN ANTONIO LIGHT* COLLECTION, THE INSTITUTE OF TEXAN CULTURES

First manager of San José Mission State Park, created in 1941, was Ethel Wilson Harris, shown in her Texas State Parks Board uniform as she rings the mission bell. Mrs. Harris, who also operated her own Mexican decorative tile company and lived on the mission grounds, retired in 1963. After renovations, her former home is to become an education center.

tuaries within a national park raised the issue of separation of church and state. This unique problem was addressed by allowing the federal government oversight of mission land and buildings, except for the churches themselves. Those would remain owned and maintained by the Catholic Church as parish churches.

A bill to create San Antonio Missions National Historical Park was about to pass in the fall of 1978 when suddenly, hours before Congress was to adjourn, it seemed doomed by last-minute congressional politics.

That news reached leaders of the San Antonio Conservation Society at 1 AM in Chicago, where they were attending a meeting of the National Trust for Historic Preservation. At once preservationists from throughout the nation swung into intense long-distance lobbying. In the hotel lounge a preservationist from Missouri watched another from Illinois come looking for a Republican from Virginia to make a call to save the bill for the missions in Texas. Twelve hours later, the bill passed.

Then funding was blocked by the executive branch until revived concern over separation of church and state could be resolved. This time a private foundation was formed to raise additional restoration funds for the mission churches and thus avoid even the appearance of any need for federal contributions to active church buildings.

At last, in 1983, more than two and a half centuries after the first Franciscan missionaries arrived in San Antonio, San Antonio Missions National Historical Park formally opened. Its initial lands comprised existing parkland donated by the city, county, state, Catholic Church and the San Antonio Conservation Society.

Since its boundaries formed islands around each of the four southern missions, and numerous private landowners ended up surrounded by park-owned land, San Antonio Missions National Historical Park became one of the most complicated park projects in the nation. The challenge of establishing good relations with neighbors in the heavily-populated area was eventually met, setting a standard for similar park development elsewhere.

By 1996, when the National Park Service completed a major visitors center at San José, the 850-acre park was attracting 1.3 million visitors each year. Already a private support group—Los Compadres, formed in 1984—had augmented government funding for park projects by raising some $1.5 million and by successfully advocating another $20 million in public and private funding.

Display themes at each mission were designed to focus on a specific aspect of mission life—at Concepción, daily religious life; San José, community and mission defense; San Juan, the mission economy of crop irrigation, livestock raising and trade; Espada, trades and crafts taught to mission Indians; and, at Espada's Rancho de las Cabras site 25 miles to the south, mission ranching.

A two-pronged effort to more clearly link downtown San Antonio with the four southern missions was well under way by the close of the 1990s. One project was building hiking and bicycle trails from the southern end of the downtown River Walk along

Archbishop Patrick Flores speaks near Mission San José's Rose Window in 1983 in ceremonies formally activating San Antonio Missions National Historical Park, created five years earlier. From left are Bishop Charles Graham and Conservation Society President Lynn Osborne Bobbitt. National Park Service Director Russell Dickenson is hidden by the podium. Next are Missions Advisory Commission Chairwoman Patsy Light, City Councilwoman Helen Dutmer and Park Service Assistant Director Mary Lou Grier.

the river to Mission Espada. The other, improving automobile access for visitors, was a greater challenge.

Although placement of the downstream missions on alternate sides of the river made sense in the eighteenth century, it created difficulties for twentieth-century travelers. Repeated attempts, many under the leadership of Henry Guerra, had been made since 1929 to establish a coherent ten-mile route linking those missions plus the Alamo. But they kept running afoul of conflicting grids of latter-day streets until 1998, when work began on the San Antonio Historic Mission Trails Project, a $35 million effort.

A lower-profile aid to understanding the missions has been augmenting mission archives owned by Bexar County by gathering copies of records long inaccessible in Mexico and elsewhere in the Old Spanish Missions Historical Research Library at San Antonio's Our Lady of the Lake University.

Through these advances in restoration, access and knowledge, four of San Antonio's missions have come full circle, capturing for future generations a sense of the hardships, sacrifices, achievements and dreams of friars and their Indian charges on the far frontier of New Spain.

The Lone Star flag of Texas flies over remains of the church of Mission San Antonio de Valero—founded with the city of San Antonio in 1718—in honor of its role in the Battle of the Alamo, fought 43 years after the mission was closed. Its signature curved gable parapet was put on the unfinished church by the U.S. Army in 1850 to cover the peak of the wooden roof added to protect quartermaster supplies being stored inside.

3. Mission San Antonio de Valero

Using information included in a 1772 Franciscan inventory of San Antonio de Valero that explained plans for the church then under construction, archeologist Jack Eaton made this drawing of how the finished church was apparently intended to look. Had the church been completed, it would have had a central dome and its Early Spanish Baroque facade would have included a third level, flanked by bell towers similar to those of the church of Mission Concepción.

At the "gateway to Spanish Texas"—across the Rio Grande from present-day Eagle Pass at today's Guerrero—Father Antonio de San Buenaventura y Olivares on March 1, 1700 founded Mission San Francisco Solano, sponsored by the Franciscan college at Querétero.

But the new mission, the third in the area, struggled in the shadow of the other two, San Juan Bautista and San Bernardo. Its assets soon seemed better used to establish a new mission as a way station for the remote missions of East Texas.

So it was that on May 1, 1718, Father Olivares took Mission San Francisco Solano's movable assets north to found such a mission with the help of several Indians he had raised from childhood at San Francisco Solano. He chose the fertile site known as San Antonio de Padua, a place he had scouted while on an expedition north in 1709.

Father Olivares located the new mission near San Pedro Springs, two miles west of the headwaters of the San Antonio River. He named it San Antonio de Valero, astutely substituting for Padua the title of the new viceroy, Balthasar Manuel de Zúñiga y Guzmán Sotomayor y Sarmiento, Marqués de Valero, who had approved the move.

A military presidio was to be founded nearby, but Father Olivares had fallen out with the man who was to establish it, Martín de Alarcón, governor of Coahuila and Texas. On May 5, 1718 Governor Alarcón, traveling separately, arrived to establish the Presidio of San Antonio de Béxar, honoring the memory of the viceroy's brother, the Duke of Béxar (Béjar), a Spanish hero who had died defending Budapest from the Turks.

A year later Mission San Antonio de Valero, its chapel built of mud, brush and straw, was moved to a better-irrigated site nearby. In 1722 the presidio was moved farther south to its permanent location beyond the west bank of the San Antonio River, forming San Antonio's Military Plaza. That fall San Antonio de Valero's temporary buildings sheltered refugees from the missions of French-plagued East Texas. One refugee, Father Francisco Hidalgo, stayed on to succeed Father Olivares.

But some Indians would not join the Payaya and Pamaya bands living at San Antonio de Valero. A leader of one holdout

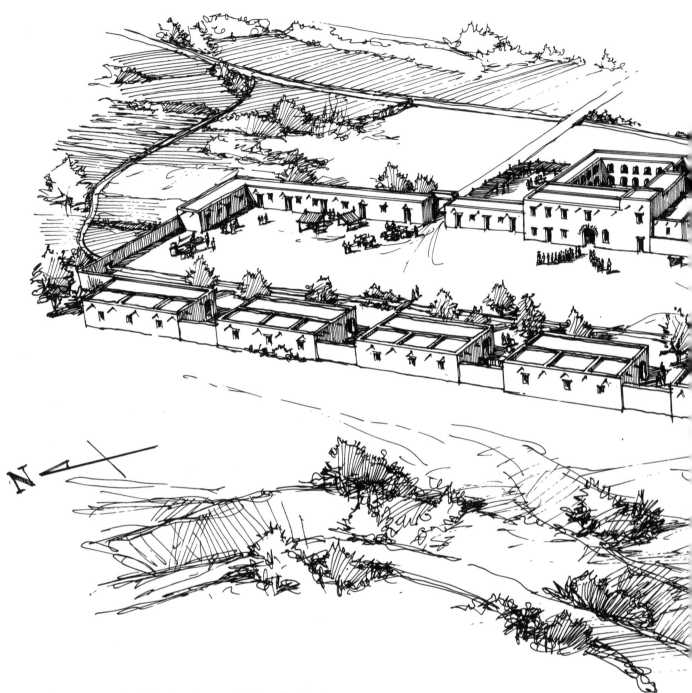

Mission San Antonio de Valero by the 1780s had reached the height of its development. Construction would soon halt on its church, right, finally roofed seven decades later by the U.S. Army. The narrow interim adobe church stands in front of the new church. To their left is the convento with its courtyard, then the granary and workshops. Lining the plaza's perimeter overlooking the San Antonio River's Great Bend are the mission Indians' quarters, which have access to water from a branch of the acequia that irrigates mission farmland.

STEVEN N. PATRICIA

tribe, a friendly Ervipiame chief with the Spanish name of Juan Rodríguez, entered San Antonio de Valero on his own. He insisted that his followers be given a separate mission run by the Querétaran Franciscans who ran San Antonio de Valero, not by the Zacatacan Franciscans who had recently established San José.

Thus, on March 12, 1722, a mission named San Francisco Xavier de Nájera was begun three miles down the river. Services were held by Father Hidalgo's assistant, Father Joseph González.

Few Indians, however, could be enticed to stay at the new mission. Chief Rodríguez himself preferred to remain at San Antonio de Valero, which he thought offered better protection against the Apaches. Four years later, Mission San Francisco Xavier de Nájera, having only a handful of converts and no permanent buildings, was merged with San Antonio de Valero.

Meanwhile, in 1724, most of San Antonio de Valero's buildings were destroyed in a hurricane. After the storm the mission was moved to the east bank of the San Antonio River. Across the river, a distance of "two gun shots" to the west, newly arrived immigrants from the Canary Islands established the Villa of San Fernando de Béxar and a parish church near the presidio in 1731.

At last in a permanent location, Mission San Antonio de Valero attracted 60 families from five tribes. Its Indian population rose to 273 even though within three years the mission's livestock herds were raided twice by Apaches.

In the Epidemic of 1739, smallpox and measles reduced the number by more than a third. But by the next winter the Indians numbered 238 and San Antonio de Valero was enjoying a reputation at the time as having the largest and best organized populace of all San Antonio missions.

The first stone for a permanent church was laid in 1744. As construction continued, the next year the 311 mission Indians—275 of them already baptized—were worshiping in the old adobe building, equipped with two confessionals, two benches and a six-foot crucifix above an altar displaying a three-foot statue of St. Anthony. In the adjoining sacristy 12 paintings and four large bells were stored for the new church.

Focal point of Mission San Antonio de Valero's church, begun by 1756, is its carved stone entry, with niches which once held the statues of saints.

Of the four former San Antonio missions whose walled compounds sheltered fighters during the turbulent years of the early nineteenth century, none approached the fame of San Antonio de Valero after its Texan defenders were annihilated in 1836. Once Mexican soldiers scaled the walls into its old compound, at left, they faced heavy fire from Texans within the former mission convento, also at left. Other defenders retreated within the walls of the unroofed mission church.

Adjoining the new two-story stone convento was a textile shop—with three looms and 20 spinning wheels—and, beside it, a granary. Indians lived in two rows of straw-roofed adobe huts lining either side of the acequia branch that crossed the mission plaza. Irrigated fields were worked by 23 yoke of oxen. On the mission ranch to the north, vaqueros used 40 horses to tend 2,300 head of cattle, 1,317 sheep and 304 goats. A stone house and stone chapel were built at the ranch.

In mid-1745 a band of 350 Apaches making a nighttime raid on San Antonio were driven off only when 100 Indians from Mission San Antonio de Valero came to the rescue. Mission defense was enhanced by three cannon in the turret at the walled mission plaza's south gate.

In 1750, the chief of San Antonio de Valero's three missionaries, Father Mariano de los Dolores y Viana, was made president

Scarcely six decades after Mission San Antonio de Valero was secularized, urbanization covered its old fields and spread into the mission compound. Hermann Lungkwitz's *Crockett Street Looking West* (1857) shows, at right, the rear of the former mission church—by then known as the Alamo. In the center of the skyline is the spire of the church of San Fernando, its priests charged with administering the former mission churches.

of the Texas Querétaran missions. San Antonio de Valero became their headquarters in place of Mission Concepción for 13 years.

By 1756, the stone church begun the decade before had collapsed. Services were held in the new stone granary while work was under way on a new church. Indians lived not in adobe huts but in stone houses—each with a door and window, beds raised above the ground, bureaus and household utensils.

Despite all the advances, however, 20 years later only 44 Indians were living there, too few to keep operating the looms or to finish the towers and roof of the church. Too, tribal identities were disappearing. Spanish was being spoken more often as Indians intermarried with settlers at the nearby villa.

When secularization was decreed for the Texas missions, the process at San Antonio de Valero occurred more quickly than at its four sister missions. In 1793 Mission San Antonio de Valero was completely closed. Its unfinished church was turned over to the diocesan priest at the parish church of San Fernando, its three farms split into tracts of seven to 21 acres.

The mission's 15 remaining Indians divided the lower farm, south of the river's Great Bend around the settlement that became known as La Villita. The upper farm, north of the bend, was split among 45 refugees from Los Adaes, the abandoned provincial

capital. The outer farm was divided among nine Spaniards, seven of them residents of the mission and two of San Antonio.

Soon San Antonio de Valero would virtually lose its identity as a Spanish mission, as its old walls began to serve as a fortress for a town on the verge of increasing turbulence.

The first soldiers to move into San Antonio de Valero were 100 members of a Spanish cavalry unit from Alamo de Parras, south of the Rio Grande. They arrived in 1803—the year the Louisiana Territory was transferred to the United States—to guard against any American invasion and to offer increased protection from Indian attacks. The troop became known as the Alamo Company, and its post became known as the Alamo. In 1805 the company made the upper level of the former convento an infirmary to which civilians were admitted, making it San Antonio's first hospital.

The old mission walls were reinforced four years later, when rumors spread of an impending invasion from the United States. In 1811 the Spanish troops helped put down a republican revolt, only to surrender the Alamo four years later—without a fight—to an invading republican force. The Alamo was abandoned, then re-garrisoned in 1817, near the close of the Mexican War of Independence.

The final buildup to the Alamo's crowning place in history came in 1835, when General Martín Perfecto de Cos's Mexican soldiers, defeated by James Bowie's Texans in the Battle of Concepción, withdrew to the Alamo. The besieged General Cos surrendered in December.

Two months later, some 187 Texans barricaded themselves in the old mission compound. The Texans, commanded by William Barret Travis, were annihilated on March 6, 1836 by a 5,000-man army under General Cos's brother-in-law, General Antonio López

In this photo taken about 1868, U.S. Army wagons load up supplies stored in the onetime Mission San Antonio de Valero church for delivery to distant forts on the Texas frontier.

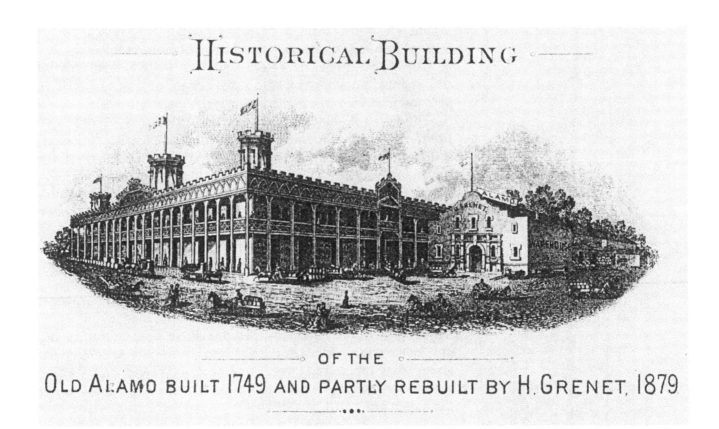

HISTORICAL BUILDING

OF THE

OLD ALAMO BUILT 1749 AND PARTLY REBUILT BY H. GRENET, 1879

Once the U.S. Army moved its supply depot from the Alamo to the new Fort Sam Houston, the Catholic Church leased the facility to a wholesale grocer who capitalized on its military fame by encasing the walls of the former mission convento in wooden battlements.

de Santa Anna, the president of Mexico, in a battle ending a 13-day siege.

The badly damaged old mission was deserted for the next ten years, as San Antonio endured the continuing traumas of Indian raids and incursions by Mexican forces into the newly independent Republic of Texas. In 1845, with Texas about to be annexed by the United States, the U.S. Army took over the Alamo as a quartermaster depot. The Army repaired its walls and screened the peak of a new roof on the old church by adding, in 1850, a rounded gable parapet, the symbol of the building ever since.

After a struggle in court with both the U.S. Army and the City of San Antonio, in 1855 the Catholic Church prevailed as owner of immediate land around the Alamo church. The old mission church and convento remained leased to the U.S. Army. Civilian buildings were built on former mission grounds nearby, and the compound's outer walls disappeared. In 1877 the Army moved to the new Fort Sam Houston, triggering dissension over the site once again.

Its tenant gone, the Catholic Church sold the former convento to a wholesale grocer, Honoré Grenet, but only leased the old mission church—to the same merchant. San Antonians, organized as the Alamo Monument Association, prevailed upon the State of Texas to buy the Alamo church in 1883 as a memorial to those killed in the battle. The state turned custody over to the City of San Antonio.

When the former convento went up for sale again, in 1903, Adina De Zavala led San Antonio's Daughters of the Republic of

Interior of the Alamo, San Antonio, Tex.

Relics from the era of the Battle of the Alamo have been housed in the old mission church since its purchase by the State of Texas in 1883. The frame roof was built over the unfinished church by the U.S. Army.

Texas chapter in lobbying for its purchase and restoration as the original Spanish mission convento.

Clara Driscoll soon led a breakaway chapter in an ultimately successful struggle to replace the city as custodian of the old church, buy the mission convento—with a loan repaid with state funds—and remove what was left of its upper story so it would not overshadow the Alamo church, made the centerpiece of a landscaped shrine to Texas heroes.

The Texas Centennial of 1936 made funds available to purchase the surrounding block. Latter-day buildings were cleared away, and an auditorium, museum/gift shop and new perimeter walls were built. A library building was added, and in 1968 the convento's remaining one-story walls were roofed for a museum.

Following 1980 excavations by the University of Texas at San Antonio's Center for Archaeological Research under Anne Fox, foundations of the west mission walls and of Indian housing were uncovered and simulated at the now-higher street level.

To provide a symbolic physical link between the river and the Alamo, a cascading waterway was built from the river through the atrium of a new hotel and up to Alamo Plaza. Dubbed the Paseo del Alamo, its narrow channels and falling water represent the life-giving flow of San Antonio's early acequia system.

Still, the debate over how to preserve the Alamo continues—should it be restored as a Spanish mission or primarily reflect its role as a battleground? How should either interpretation deal with

In 1931 Alamo Plaza anchored the eastern end of downtown San Antonio. Curbs lining grassy areas in the old mission plaza offered prime parking spots. Within five years came the centennial of the fall of the Alamo and funds to purchase and clear the block around the church and convento area as an enlarged shrine to Texas liberty.

Although the face of Alamo Plaza continues to change, the old mission church remains an obligatory stop for visitors to San Antonio. They included, in 1991, Queen Elizabeth II, being shown a diorama of Mission San Antonio de Valero by local historian Henry Guerra as Prince Philip and Alamo Curator Charles Long, far right, look on.

Foundations of the Indian barracks of Mission San Antonio de Valero are replicated (foreground) at street level, several feet above excavations of the original foundations. Sets of twin concrete posts guard each side of a city street through the original San Antonio de Valero compound, the last of San Antonio's Spanish mission plazas still crossed by latter-day public roads.

the site, encroached upon as it is by streets and commercial buildings?

Though these issues remain unresolved, in recent decades municipal beautification efforts have included marking the line of the mission's long-gone outer walls, closing one of the streets that bisect the onetime mission plaza and then closing another directly in front of the church, to honor the sanctity of what could be the burial place of Indian converts who died centuries before, within the walls of Mission San Antonio de Valero.

4. Mission Nuestra Señora de la Purísima Concepción de Acuña

The new East Texas Mission Nuestra Señora de la Purísima Concepción de los Hainais was made headquarters for the reestablished Querétaran missions, chosen by the leader of the effort, the Franciscan missionary and chronicler Father Isidro Félix de Espinosa.

It was founded in 1716 in the Angelina River valley west of present-day Nacogdoches in the homeland of the Hainai Indians, one of the chief groups of Caddoans in the confederacy known by the Spaniards as Tejas.

After a quick start the mission suffered two years without supplies from Mexico, then a drought and a famine that reduced inhabitants to hunting crows.

"True, the color, flavor and toughness of this meat were quite repugnant," wrote Father Espinosa of the birds. "But hunger made it so appetizing that for the greater part of the year crow's meat was one of our most delicious dishes."

Next came an epidemic in which hundreds of Indians died and then, in 1719, an outbreak of border conflict with the French. That fall the Spaniards retreated to San Antonio. They returned to rededicate the salvaged buildings of Mission Concepción on August 8, 1721.

Soon after, Father Espinosa returned to Mexico to head the Franciscan college at Querétaro, leaving Concepción's resident priest and organizer, Father Gabriel de Vergara, as president of the Texas Querétaran missions. At Concepción, Father Vergara in 1729 convened a meeting to oppose closing of the nearby presidio, which offered the missions some measure of military protection. But the protest was to no avail.

With support from Father Espinosa in Querétaro and with permission from the viceroy in Mexico City, Concepción and its two neighboring Querétaran missions moved west to the Colorado River and, finally, to San Antonio.

On March 5, 1731, Mission Concepción was reestablished on the east bank of the San Antonio River, halfway between the Querétaran Mission San Antonio de Valero and the Zacatecan

Facing page: Dedicated in 1755, Mission Concepción's church is the nation's oldest unreconstructed Spanish church.

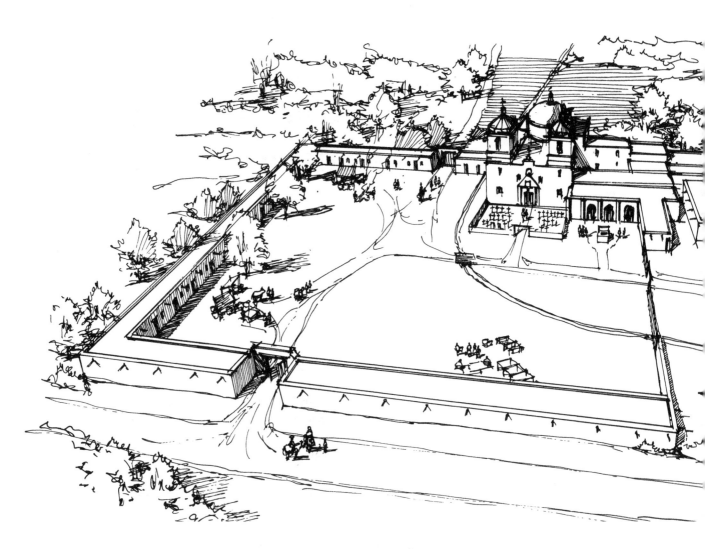

Auxiliary buildings of Mission Concepción adjoined its twin-towered church,
dedicated in 1755. On the second story of the convento beside the church was the office
of the Father President who supervised Querétaran missions in Texas. To the right
stood the granary and workshops. Mission Indians lived in rooms along the perimeter
walls. The quarry in the right foreground provided rock for construction.

Mission San José y San Miguel de Aguayo on the site of the short-lived San Francisco Xavier de Nájera.

In San Antonio the ending of the mission's name was changed from "los Hainais" to "de Acuña" in honor of the viceroy who permitted the move—Juan de Acuña, Marqués de Casafuerte. The reborn Concepción, like its predecessor, was made headquarters for the province's Querétaran missions, an honor it kept except for the 13 years the designation was held by Mission San Antonio de Valero.

To standardize spoken communication, Father Vergara sought to make Palajat, the language of the major tribe at Concepción, the basic tongue of the mission. He published a Pajalat-Spanish glossary and began a manual for missionaries in Palajat.

Both Father Vergara, who left to head the college in Querétaro in 1737, and his successor at Concepción, Father Benito Fernández de Santa Ana, deplored military reprisals against raiding Apaches, believing instead that establishing missions specifically for the Apaches would bring peace. The conciliatory approach urged by the two mission priests later, in 1749, facilitated a formal peace agreement—though of no lasting effect—with the Apaches.

As Mission Concepción grew, temporary wooden and thatched-roofed adobe buildings were replaced by buildings of stone cut in a quarry just outside the mission's walls. Work was disrupted when the Epidemic of 1739 cut its Indian population of 250 in half, but the mission soon recovered. Thanks to new converts from the countryside, the mission's Indians again numbered more than 200 by 1745. By 1756, Mission Concepción had baptized 792 Indians and given 558 Christian burials.

The whitewashed walls of the Father President's second floor convento office, lit by a scalloped window, were once adorned with colorful frescoes.

Concepción's mission Indian artists framed doorways with frescoes of imaginary stone and did other wall designs and borders. Remnants within the convento were restored by an internationally sponsored group of art restoration specialists in 1988.

At this point, each season Concepción's Indians were harvesting 800 bushels of corn from eight bushels of seed and 24 bushels of beans from one and three-fifths bushels of seed, plus melons, watermelons and pumpkins. Thirty yoke of oxen worked the mission fields, irrigated by an acequia fed by a dam on the San Antonio River near present-day Presa ("Dam") Street two and a half miles to the north. On mission ranchlands 30 miles east were 900 head of cattle, 300 sheep and 100 horses.

Mission Concepción's cruciform church was begun by Father Fernández. It was completed by his successor, Father Francisco Cayetano del Aponte y Lis and dedicated on December 8, 1755. Its facade was painted with geometric designs, its twin towers topped by crosses of iron and weather vanes. Above the entrance

Visitors to Mission Concepcion can still take the original arched stone stairway to the second floor office of the Father Presidents who supervised Querétaran missions in Texas.

The irregular position of Mission Concepción's baptismal font in relation to the unrestored fresco above it suggests that it was installed some time after the earliest years of the church, when a free-standing font was in use. Similarity of this font's sculptural detail to work at Mission San Antonio de Valero leads some historians to speculate that the font was moved to Concepción after San Antonio de Valero—the Alamo—was secularized in 1793.

Facing page: The original stone shield over the door to Concepción's church bears the Latin initials "M" and "AVE," standing for Ave Maria, or Hail Mary. To its left is the sculpted coat of arms of the Franciscans, to its right a design symbolizing Christ's wounds.

was carved, apparently in the 1890s, a Latin inscription translated as "To its Patroness and Princess, with these arms this mission gives honor and defends the doctrine of her purity."

A cupola brought light to the stone altar table, on which stood a three-foot statue of the Virgin Mary. Each transept had its altar and framed painting, and sanctuary walls were lined with 14 paintings of the Stations of the Cross. At the rear was a choir loft with a vaulted ceiling. At the base of one bell tower, an altar dedicated to St. Michael was adorned with a painting of the Holy Archangel. The room at the base of the other was a baptistry.

In the adjoining sacristy, three walnut chests stored accoutrements for the Mass. Workshops adjoined the barrel-vaulted convento, its walls and ceiling painted with frescoes by Indian artists.

As Indian raids took their toll on all of San Antonio's missions, Concepción's ranch was closed when Comanches made off with the horses in 1767. Yet the mission still did well, attracting Indians from diverse tribes. Of the 173 Indians at Concepción in 1772 were 75 Palajat, 48 Manos de Perro, 18 Tacame, 18

Although Concepción's unused church billeted Mexican revolutionaries, Republic of Texas soldiers and then U.S. Army troops, and was also used as a barn, the building remained intact. This pastoral scene was engraved for *Harper's New Monthly Magazine* in 1877.

Toareque and 14 Sanipao. They lived in two dozen houses within the mission plaza's stone walls, whose three gates were armed with two small bronze cannons.

But by 1783 Concepción's Indian population was down to 87. Even members of minority tribes began calling themselves Palajats as original identities slipped away.

As Concepción's secularization began in 1794, its lands were distributed among the 38 remaining Indians and its church buildings placed in the care of the missionary at San José. Spanish settlers moved in, by 1809 numbering 32 compared to 21 Indians. A decade later services were no longer held in the church.

Even before its secularization was completed in 1824, the region's political instability shook Concepción. In 1813 forces of Mexican revolutionary leader Bernardo Gutiérrez de Lara set up temporary headquarters within its walls. The Texas Revolutionary War Battle of Concepción was fought in 1835 in the old mission fields, when 90 Texans under James Bowie and James W. Fannin Jr. repulsed a 400-man Mexican cavalry force under Martín Perfecto de Cos. The Texans camped in the Concepción compound, damaging some buildings.

Under the Republic of Texas, county officials in 1840 put up for sale "public rock" at the mission, specifically exempting from public use the stone from the church, then being used as a barn. The church was made a supply depot by the U.S. Army during the Mexican War.

Although the interior of Mission Concepción's church remained protected, by the early 1880s the area outside was adapted for farm use. A makeshift building was added near the entrance, while the second-story office to the right of the dome got a tin roof. An open-sided room of the old convento, right, sheltered a buckboard.

Future President Theodore Roosevelt, center, joins the growing number of tourists at Mission Concepción in 1898 during a break in training his Rough Riders at nearby Riverside Park, now Roosevelt Park.

Facing page: The earliest known photo of the interior of Mission Concepción's church, above left, shows the refurbishing of 1861, which made the church once again usable for religious services. Appearance of the chancel, above right, changed dramatically in 1887, when a mural reflected the church's new dedication to Our Lady of Lourdes.

By 1906 the mission compound, below, was again showing signs of neglect, leading to the refurbishing of 1911 which also removed the mural.

The outlook for the old mission began to improve in 1855, when Brother Andrew Edel, who had helped found a predecessor of St. Mary's University, set up a farm on church-owned land at Concepción. It soon was feeding a Society of Mary school nearby. In 1860 Bishop Jean Marie Odin bought Concepción's convento and turned it over with the church to the Society of Mary, which cleaned, repaired and reopened the church for services on May 28, 1861. The farm was closed in 1869 and its lands were leased to farmers, but the church was still tended to. In 1887 it was again repaired, and dedicated to Our Lady of Lourdes.

Title to Concepción went back to the bishop in 1911 and its surroundings were transformed. Hoping for eventual return of the Franciscans, Bishop John W. Shaw had the area landscaped, and refurbished the church and reopened it in 1913. On a newly-acquired tract across the road to the west, St. Peter's-St. Joseph's Orphanage was built by the Sisters of Charity of the Incarnate Word. On a new adjacent tract to the northeast, St. John's Seminary, to be open for a half-century, was completed in 1920.

Federal relief workers began the first general restoration and archaeological efforts at Concepción in the 1930s. Forty years later a major project uncovered remains of the orginal convento, adobe church, granary, workshops and three rows of Indian quarters.

A short-lived frame house incongruously abuts outbuildings at Mission Concepción after the renovations of 1911, when the church was repaired for services and surrounding land was leased to farmers.

Since 1965 interior work at Concepción, and Catholic Archdiocesesan mission church restoration in general, has been directed by the architectural firm of Ford Powell and Carson, under supervision of O'Neil Ford and, later, of Carolyn Peterson. A small visitors center was built with the aid of funds raised by Los Compadres, the park's independent support group. The road passing by the front of the church was rerouted around the site of the perimeter walls.

Los Compadres also funded restoration of damaged eighteenth-century frescoes on the walls of Concepción's convento. The team of conservators from San Antonio, New York and Italy was directed by the International Council of Monuments and Sites and by the International Center for the Study of Preservation of Restoration of Cultural Property. Some of the specialists had helped restore the ceiling of the Vatican's Sistine Chapel.

Conservators removing layers of salt deposits that had seeped through the vaulted convento library limestone ceiling revealed that what had been seen as only a single "Eye of God" was actually part of a round mestizo face with a moustache, goatee and a halo with radiating sunlike rays. To traditional native motifs symbolizing water, sun and earth, Franciscans had seen that Indian artists added human features in the European artistic tradition to link the Christian concept of a single omnipotent God with the familiar power of the sun.

By 1920, the three-story red brick building of St. John's Seminary, above right, had brought new life to the grounds of Mission Concepción, the vaulted ceiling of its convento extending from the south tower still intact. At right, a procession from the seminary in 1932 passes the church on its way to an outdoor Mass at St. Peter's-St. Joseph's Orphanage across the road.

With the road that cut through the onetime mission plaza now re-routed around the
site of the old mission walls to offer this vista, Mission Concepción's church and
surviving convento buildings stand once again in an open setting, conducive
to contemplation in the convento's original cloisters (*facing page*).

5. Mission San José y San Miguel de Aguayo

Facing page: Nearly a half-century of preservation efforts culminated in 1948 with final restoration of Mission San José's baroque entrance facade to its original appearance. A figure of St. Joseph, the mission's patron saint, stands above the oval window. At its right is St. Francis of Assisi, founder of the Franciscan order, and to its left St. Dominic, friend of St. Francis. Above the wooden doors—copies of the lost originals—is a relief of the Virgin of Guadalupe below a shell symbolizing the sacrament of baptism. On either side of the doors are statues of the Virgin Mary's parents, St. Joachim and St. Anne, with the hearts above the statues representing the hearts of Joseph and Mary.

After Querétaran Franciscans founded Mission San Antonio de Valero, some of the tribes that were unfriendly with Indians in the new mission refused to enter.

Father Antonio Margil de Jesús, president of the Franciscan college in Zacatecas and veteran of missionary work in Yucatán, Costa Rica and Guatemala, saw the solution as a second San Antonio mission, run by Zacatecan Franciscans rather than by those from Querétaro. The governor of Coahuila and Texas, the Marqués de San Miguel de Aguayo, agreed, and on January 22, 1720 he authorized its founding. He financed the venture as well. Father Margil named the new mission San José and appended the title of his benefactor.

San José's original site, chosen by the captain of the Presidio of San Antonio de Béxar, was three miles south of San Antonio on the east bank of the San Antonio River. There, more than 200 Indians were gathered in temporary huts around a square. On it faced a temporary chapel and quarters for two missionaries, Agustín Patrón, who was reassigned after a year, and Miguel Núñez de Haro, who guided San José until his death in 1752.

Two years later, when the short-lived Mission San Francisco Xavier de Nájera was also established upstream on the east bank, San José was moved to the west bank. San José grew, with 300 Indians worshiping in its adobe church.

But disease bred by river water at the new lowland site caused San José to suffer the sharpest of all local missions' losses during the Epidemic of 1739. Deaths, plus runaways, cut the number of its Indians to 49. San José's two priests also became ill. But they recovered to pursue the defectors and also gather some potential converts, raising the number by 200 by the end of the next year.

To avoid disease, San José was moved away from the river to higher ground, to its third and permanent site. In 1758 the provincial governor could enthusiastically report to the viceroy that San José had baptized 964 Indians, half of them at the new location, and that priests had officiated at 145 marriages and 466 burials.

By this time, the new adobe church with its belltower dominated a square with a two-story stone convento, 84 stone houses for Indians, a granary holding 4,000 bushels of corn, workshops, a sugar mill for making cane syrup and cones of brown sugar, a cemetery and quarters for three Spanish soldiers. Irrigation ditches

Father Antonio Margil de Jesús, leader of the Franciscan college in Zacatecas, did missionary work in Mexico and Central America before becoming involved in Texas, where he founded Mission San José, the most successful mission in the province. This statue of Father Margil, who has been proposed to the Vatican for sainthood, was placed at Mission San Juan Capistrano in 1995.

leading from the mission acequia watered farmlands worked by 30 yoke of oxen.

Twenty-five miles south, San José's ranch had 3,376 sheep and 1,500 head of branded cattle, despite losing 2,000 head of cattle to Apache raids during the previous nine years. Continuing raids caused mission buildings to be enclosed in the 1760s by gated perimeter walls 611 feet on each side, with corner towers.

On March 19, 1768, the feast day of St. Joseph, the mission's patron saint, Father José Gaspar Solís from Zacatecas blessed the foundations of a new church on the site of the adobe church. Father Pedro de Ramírez supervised its building of limestone quarried at Concepción. The sacristy, finished in 1777, was used for services while the sanctuary and one tower moved toward completion; whether a second tower was planned is as yet undetermined.

Even before the new church was begun, Father Solís thought San José "so pretty and in such a flourishing condition, both materially and spiritually, that I cannot find words or figures with which to express its beauty." Indeed, travel writers by the nineteenth century were referring to San José as the "Queen of the Missions of New Spain."

But as its church was being built, the magnificent mission's decline had begun. Resident Indians declined from 350 in 1768 to 275 in 1777 and to 138 in 1789, though still numbering more than half those remaining at all San Antonio missions. Too, Indians were increasingly adapting to European ways. As their consumption of wheat products approached that of traditional maize dishes, a small mill to grind wheat into flour was built outside the northern mission wall in the 1790s by the young priest José Manuel Pedrajo. Water from the acequia turned a horizontal millwheel underground.

About the same time, what many consider to be the finest Spanish colonial sculpture in Spanish North America was carved in native limestone to frame San José's sacristy window. Despite a romantic story that first surfaced in the 1920s regarding its completion by surveyor Pedro Huizar in memory of a lost love named Rose or Rosa, the window's carving has been linked instead to native craftsmen trained at the Franciscan college in Zacatecas.

It is also more likely that the Rose Window was dedicated to St. Rose—Santa Rosa—of Lima, Peru, whose feast day is on Pentecost, when priests display the Eucharist to the people. The priest conducting Mass in the sacristy would have climbed the inside step to the window's opening—which faces south toward Lima—and displayed the Eucharist to throngs gathered outside the window.

By 1815, San José housed only 49 Indians. Sixty Spanish residents lived nearby. Before being finally closed nine years later, San José was caught up in the region's turmoil. Soldiers had intermittently fortified themselves within its walls since 1813, when local republicans rebelled against royalist authority. Sculpture on the church facade was used for target practice by soldiers when San José served as a supply depot during the Mexican War.

Bishop Jean Marie Odin, having successfully reasserted church ownership of the old missions, sought to revive San José by bringing

The Spanish steps to Mission San José's church belltower were hewn from single blocks of wood by Indian workers who lived in quarters along the perimeter walls, shown lower right with a reconstructed bread oven. Quarters reconstructed along the north wall, upper right, may have been those of soldiers stationed at the mission.

Remodeling of San José's convento as a monastery was left uncompleted by Benedictine priests from Pennsylvania who lived at the mission from 1859 to 1868.

in Benedictines from Latrobe, Pennsylvania, in 1859. The Benedictines held services in the church and began reconstructing the convento at the rear, adding the distinctive pointed Gothic arches in a project that remained unfinished after they left in 1868, the year part of the church's north wall collapsed.

Indiana's Holy Cross Fathers of Notre Dame, hoping to make the old mission a retreat center for the University of Notre Dame, were in charge of San José for 12 years beginning in 1873. A year later, during Christmas Eve services in the sacristy, the church's dome collapsed, leaving the church roofless. Some services continued to be held in the decaying sacristy, entered only from the outside since the fallen debris blocked entrance from the sanctuary.

Now the derelict church was also falling victim to the increasing numbers of tourists, who had San José high on their list of places to see. In 1890 one local writer, William Corner, was complaining about "the wanton mutilitation of the sculptures of the Missions by thoughtless relic hunters. . . . At San José whole figures have been stolen and others made headless; the fine old cedar paneled doors of this Mission were entirely wrecked and carried away piecemeal."

For the next four decades San José would be the primary rallying point for those seeking to preserve San Antonio's missions. The overcoming of seemingly insurmountable obstacles in Mission San José's transformation from ruin to the restored keystone of a National Historical Park is a saga in some ways as heroic as San José's original creation and growth on a hostile frontier.

Tourists climbed the belfry stairs to line the edge of the tower for the earliest known photograph of the San José mission church, taken as early as 1854. The dome would not collapse until 1873.

The first to work toward mission preservation for the public was the single-minded president of San Antonio's Daughters of the Republic of Texas chapter, Adina De Zavala, a schoolteacher and devout Catholic. With permission from Bishop John Anthony Forest, Miss De Zavala and her cohorts in mid-1902 launched a national letter-writing campaign to restore Mission San José, which they wrote was "considered the most beautiful on the continent."

The drive brought in only a few hundred dollars, the largest contributions being $25 from the Texas Chapter of the Colonial Dames of America and $50 from Helen Gould, daughter of the late railroad magnate Jay Gould. Nevertheless, with the aid of materials donated by local businesses, workmen were hired to put up a six-foot fence to protect the doorless San José church from stray cows wandering the road that ran beside it, across the foundations of the fast-disappearing mission plaza's walls.

Also, the cemetery was fenced, cracks in the church walls were filled with mortar and workmen spent three days bracing the entrance to hold the cracking sculptured facade in place. The head of one family living in the old granary that faced the church was paid to keep an eye on things. To greet tourists, a board over a gate in the fence was later painted, "The Mission San Jose."

San José's three-domed sacristy, completed in 1777, could be entered a century later only through its exterior rear door, above, since debris from the nave's fallen roof blocked the scalloped side entrance into the church. By 1890 a showcase with relics, right, sat in the unusable doorway as the sacristy, though plagued by leaks and flaking plaster, continued to be used for services. An original mission bell hangs in the frame to the left of the showcase, and a decorated fabric is stretched above the altar. At far left is the inside of the Rose Window, showing the step the priest would mount on the feast day of St. Rose to display the Eucaharist through the window to mission Indians novitiates who could not yet be admitted inside the church, but who gathered outside.

RIGHT: THE INSTITUTE OF TEXAN CULTURES, COURTESY MRS. ROBERT M. AYRES

San José's mission plaza had virtually disappeared by the turn of the century, thanks to a public road which cut through the vanished mission walls past the surviving granary and church (*facing page*) and to other roadways and new buildings. In 1902 the church was finally fenced from cows who wandered in from their home in the old granary.

By 1918 the church interior, above, had been cleared of debris from the fallen roof and dome, reopening the indoor entry to the sacristy, left foreground. Some of the stones were used to rebuild part of the north wall, far right. Also, the front entrance and facade were rebraced.

Still, deterioration continued. In 1903 the stone turret enclosing the belltower's spiral stairway burst, strewing the hand-hewn hardwood steps of Bois d'Arc on the ground. Three years later nearby residents complained that the new fence hindered their movements in the area, and the county ordered the fence removed.

A decade later the Catholic Church gathered donations to clear debris from the sanctuary, partially reconstruct the north wall and, in 1918, to reopen the refurbished sacristy with funding from civic leader Ethel Tunstall Drought. Mrs. Drought also funded rebuilding the belfry stairway turret using the original steps that she had rescued and kept at her home after the original turret collapsed.

Despite the good intentions of Adina De Zavala's new group, the Texas Historical and Landmarks Association, for "restoration and conservation of all the missions of Texas along the lines of such work in California," the next substantive move to preserve San José was led by Rena Maverick Green. Area Congressman John Nance Garner thought Mrs. Green's goal of obtaining a missions national park was unlikely to draw sufficient congressional support, and he urged her to pursue creation of a state park instead.

Soon after San José's tower collapsed in the predawn
darkness of March 9, 1928, the Catholic archdiocese
had scaffolding up to rebuild it. Federally funded relief
workers later poured concrete to restore the roof,
although the dome was left unfinished, right, when
questions of separation of church and state
caused the government to halt its work.

Preservation and restoration of the original San José compound was a prime goal of the San Antonio Conservation Society when it was founded in 1924. The group's subsequent piecemeal purchase of most of the mission plaza included the roofless granary, left. Its reconstruction was completed in 1933.

As head of the local Daughters of the Republic of Texas missions committee, on a spring afternoon in 1924 Mrs. Green drew Texas Governor Pat Neff and the entire State Parks Board to San José to show them first hand the mission's potential as a state park.

At a dinner that night, a San Diego Chamber of Commerce official in town to promote the Old Spanish Trail Highway from California through San Antonio to Florida—the present-day route of Interstate 10—was assigned to speak on "what California would do with the San Antonio missions if they were located there." He reported that his instructions were, "Bring the missions home with you."

As public awareness of the plight of the still decaying mission complexes broadened, Mrs. Green became a co-founder of the San Antonio Conservation Society. In the summer of 1924, the four-month-old Conservation Society targeted the rescue of San José as a primary goal.

Mrs. Green strategized with longtime California mission preservationist Charles F. Lummis, but found San Antonio's archdiocese unwilling to grant the sort of leases that Lummis's group had obtained from the church in California. The archbishop quickly ordered rebuilding of the still roofless church's belltower when it collapsed in 1928, but he told local preservationists that otherwise "the church has no funds for preservation or restoration, but only for saving souls."

Nor were state officials willing to seek the type of public bond issues being passed in California to establish mission parks.

So the San Antonio Conservation Society set out on its own to buy the small tracts that checkerboarded the original compound of Mission San José. Using borrowed funds, by the end of 1929 the society owned land on three sides of the now roofless granary and a third of the building itself, which the ladies revered as the oldest structure standing in Texas. Their husbands, cajoled into guaranteeing the loans, thought it merely "a pile of rocks."

The Spanish Missions of San Antonio

Reconstruction foreman Jo Mahavier, above, holds a newly uncovered spoon bearing the emblem of the Franciscan order as work on San José progresses. Latter-day intrusions loom out of place along southeast walls near San José's present main gate (*facing page*, above) as, at the southwest gate (*facing page*, below) Indian barracks are rebuilt.

In 1931 the society bought the remaining section of the granary from the last holdout when he was arrested on charges of gambling and bootlegging and needed money quickly to stay out of jail.

A few months later, the society sold a newly purchased tract just outside the former mission walls to the Catholic Church for a friary for the Franciscans, who were returning to San José after 107 years. Then the state was persuaded to keep a new highway from crossing over newly-rediscovered perimeter walls.

Thanks to Depression relief efforts, the Conservation Society could enlist publicly paid workers for a restoration effort, undertaken by a succession of government agencies—the Federal Emergency Relief Administration, then the Civil Works Administration and finally the Works Progress Administration, all aided by local architect Harvey P. Smith.

Workmen rebuilt the mission walls and Indian quarters, cleared buildings from the plaza and rerouted the criss-crossing roadways, newly closed by the county. Engineer and artist Ernst Schuchard analyzed paint fragments and deciphered the colorful original designs on the church facade. Thanks to partial funding from the National Society of Colonial Dames in Texas he could help reconstruct the mission mill, its buried remains discovered by chance near the sloping ground north of the mission walls, where federal workers built an outdoor theater dubbed the Huisache Bowl.

In 1933 the Conservation Society leased the cool, vaulted interior of the granary to Ethel Wilson Harris as a shop for her decorative Mexican art tile company, known through most of its history

San José's church and granary, left center, were still roofless and roads and driveways looped around its former mission plaza in 1931, the year the U-shaped Franciscan friary, upper right, was completed behind the church.

as Mission Crafts. Artisans were installed in leased rooms of the rebuilt Indian quarters, and Mrs. Harris moved into an apartment in quarters along the north wall. Until she built a kiln on mission grounds, much work—now nationally recognized for its quality—was fired under contract with the nearby San José Potteries.

The two operations made San Antonio the center of the state's decorative tile and pottery industry, though their work is sometimes confused with that produced in San José, California.

To celebrate the plaza's completion, on June 14, 1936, the Conservation Society threw "A Night in Spain" on the plaza. The mission church, however, was still unfinished. Work halted partway through rebuilding its dome when the Works Progress Administration determined that federally-funded work on a church-owned building violated separation of church and state.

That fall the Catholic Church, with the aid of $20,000 in Texas Centennial funds, resumed work on its own. It dedicated the nearly restored church in the spring of 1937 with a Solemn Pontifical Mass celebrated by Archbishop Arthur J. Drossaerts.

To attract visitors there were mission tours, weekend craft demonstrations by artisans and, on summer evenings, outdoor historical dramas in the Huisache Bowl. "A Night in Spain" became the Conservation Society's annual Indian Harvest Festival, which

San José Mission was transformed by 1941, the year it became a state park. Both church and granary were restored, perimeter walls in the style of the originals enclosed a cleared and replanted mission plaza and a new state highway, foreground, had been rerouted away from the complex in the nick of time.

later moved downtown to La Villita and evolved into A Night in Old San Antonio, the nation's largest single fund-raising event for historic preservation. The Spanish miracle play *Los Pastores* was performed each Christmas season.

Extended negotiations among the three mission compound property owners—the Catholic Church, the Conservation Society and Bexar County, the right-of-way owner—culminated in 1941 with creation of Mission San José State Park and its naming as a National Historic Site. Ethel Wilson Harris, the decorative tile maker, was named park superintendent.

As part of the agreement, the National Park Service, brought into discussions six years earlier by then-Congressman Maury Maverick, was to help guide future preservation by providing plans, supervision and some funds, even as efforts continued to make all four southern missions a national park.

Finally, after more than three decades of starts and stops, a national historical park was established in 1978. Five years later, in 1983, representatives of a host of local, state and national secular and religious entities gathered in the old plaza near the sacristy window of the church of Mission San José y San Miguel de Aguayo for the official signing of the cooperative agreements fully activating San Antonio Missions National Historical Park.

Completion of San José's plaza restoration in 1936 inspired the San Antonio Conservation Society to throw a midsummer "A Night In Spain," below, precursor of the society's "A Night In Old San Antonio" Fiesta-time extravaganza. The next spring, an opening in the partly-restored dome gave a photographer a unique vantage point for the Solemn Pontifical Mass rededicating the church, an unfinished floor and wall visible near the altar. The restored nave (*facing page*) now serves an independent parish.

Once restored, with its church and courtyard again surrounded by perimeter
walls (*facing page*), Mission San José
became the site of numerous activities.
Native crafts returned to the mission
after nearly a century and a half when
Ethel Wilson Harris leased some
restored Indian quarters, above, for
artisans of her Mission Crafts workshop. Plays, including mission-related
historical dramas, were performed
at an outdoor theater, right.

Negotiations concluded in 1941 made Mission San José both a State Park and a National Historic Site. At the table are, from left, National Park Service Historic Section Director Aubrey Neasham, Bexar County Judge Charles W. Anderson, Archbishop Robert E. Lucey, State Parks Board Director Frank Quinn and San Antonio Conservation Society President Amanda Taylor.

The Spanish miracle play *Los Pastores*, sponsored by the San Antonio Conservation Society and San Antonio Missions National Historical Park, is performed at San José each Christmas season.

Mission San José's sacristy "Rose Window" is believed to have been dedicated to St. Rose of Lima Peru. As Mass was held in the sacristy, the mission priest would display the Eucharist through the window to those gathered outside. The carving, by natives trained in Zacatecas, is often considered the finest example of Spanish colonial sculpture in the United States.

6. Mission San Juan Capistrano

San Juan Capistrano began its first life as Mission San José de los Nazonis, founded in 1716 to serve the Nazoni and Nadaco Indians north of present-day Nacogdoches. Like the Querétarans' two other East Texas missions, three years later it was abandoned in the face of the French and reestablished in 1721, only to relocate to the present-day Austin area in 1730 and then to the banks of the San Antonio River, where it was reestablished on March 5, 1731.

To avoid confusion with its new neighbor two and a half miles upstream, Mission San José y San Miguel de Aguayo, Mission San José de los Nazonis was renamed in honor of a recently canonized saint, John of Capistrano, an Italian theologian, Franciscan and inquisitor whose eloquent preaching recruited critically needed peasant troops for a victory over the Turks at Belgrade in 1456.

Life in San Juan's first years was made difficult by raiding Apaches, who in 1736 killed two mission Indian women not far outside the mission compound. After the new provincial governor the next year withdrew two of the three soldiers who gave San Juan what protection it did have, mission affairs were thrown into chaos.

When San Juan's missionary priest objected to the move, the governor drew the mission Indians into the disagreement. Discipline broke down, mission life ground to a halt and most Indians departed. Many returned six months later when a new governor and a new priest patched things up, only to have the Epidemic of 1739 combine with the usual desertions to reduce San Juan's Indian population from 218 to 66.

But six years later, San Juan nevertheless housed 41 Indian families comprising 163 persons, 113 of them baptized. The mission was making do with a straw-roofed chapel of brush plastered with mud, its tower having two bells. On the altar was a three-fourths life-size statue of Our Lady of Sorrows, flanked by smaller images of the infant Jesus and St. Joseph and standing below a gilt-framed oil painting of St. John of Capistrano. The chapel also had a confessional, a copper baptismal font and four sets of colored vestments.

Around the mission plaza were Indian quarters, a small stone friary, a stone granary and workshops. The farm produced 1,280

Facing page: San Juan Capistrano's chapel stands across the plaza from the ruins of the unfinished mission church, begun about 1760, which was to include an octagonal sacristy, part of its foundation visible in the left foreground.

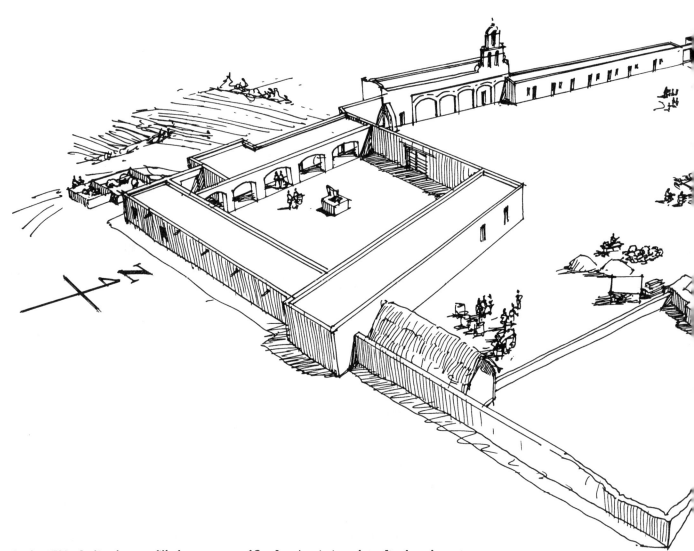

In the 1780s, Indian houses filled one corner of San Juan's mission plaza. Its chapel, built on the foundations of the old granary, was serving as the mission church in the 1780s, since across the plaza the new church with its octagonal sacristy was still under construction. The convento compound, left, was entered through a gate into the plaza, since the gate in the exterior wall, far left, had been walled up two decades before. Outside, at the far left, corrals held some mission livestock.

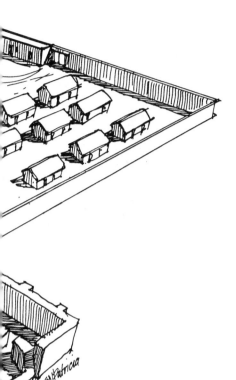

bushels of corn in good years, and the ranch had 865 head of cattle, 304 sheep, 270 goats and 36 horses.

As Mission San Juan Capistrano prospered, by 1756 its two missionaries were holding services in a long, narrow, wood-roofed stone chapel with five recessed arches on the side facing the plaza. The chapel was topped by an *espadaña*, an open belfry in two tiers with space for three bells. Its altar held three three-foot statues, one of its patron saint in the center. Six years later the chapel had three altars, the center one holding the statue of St. John of Capistrano. Two side altars held statues of Jesus and of Our Lady of Rosario.

The sacristy featured a statue of Our Lady of Sorrows wearing a dress and a silver cross and holding a sword, and it held chests with 21 vestments of silk and damask and a silver-lined baptismal font. Since 1731 there had been 847 Indians baptized at San Juan, and 645 had been given a Christian burial.

Immediately south of the chapel, at the mission plaza's southwest corner, were two convento buildings—one housing a textile shop with three looms—and a long stone granary. They formed two sides of a walled compound entered from the outside, until the 1760s, through a heavy gate. The granary served briefly as a chapel, while across the plaza work began on its replacement—a large, permanent stone church with an adjoining octagonal-walled sacristy.

In 1762, preparations were being made for the Indians' thatched-roof adobe houses in the plaza's northeast quadrant to be replaced with stone houses. There were 203 Indians in 51 families, most of them Orejon, Sayopin, Pamaque and Piquique. The

San Juan's convento courtyard area can again be entered from outside the mission compound through a southwest corner gateway, once sealed.

Mission San Juan Capistrano's chapel was reroofed and repaired for services in 1877 by the parish priest, Father Francis Bouchu, before he moved to Mission Espada across the river.

mission was still defended by three Spanish soldiers armed with swivel guns.

Within ten years, however, San Juan's Indian population was dropping sharply, as was that of other missions. On July 9, 1771, San Juan's chief missionary, Father Mariano de los Dolores, set out for the Texas coast in search of runaways and new converts. With him were several mission Indians and 30 soldiers commanded by the captain of the San Antonio presidio. A month later the expedition was back with 107 Indians. Two-thirds were assigned to San Juan, the others to Concepción and Espada.

But the long-term decline could not be reversed. In 1789 San Juan's Indians numbered only 58, too few to complete the stone church and octagonal sacristy started some 30 years before.

When secularization began in 1794, San Juan was made a subsidiary of Mission San Francisco de la Espada across the river. In 1815 San Juan served 15 Indians plus 50 Spaniards who settled nearby. When the mission closed ten years later, the chapel was turned over to San Antonio's parish church of San Fernando. Mission lands were auctioned off.

In 1858 a French immigrant lay priest, Francis Bouchu, was assigned by the priest at San Fernando to serve a broad farming area south of San Antonio. He settled at Mission San Juan, perhaps building the house which now survives in ruins on the eastern wall of the mission compound. By 1877 he had reroofed and repaired the chapel for services.

Father Bouchu, who began dividing his time between San Juan and Espada, moved permanently to Espada in 1885. The next year

In a surreal view taken about 1895, three men lounge on the walls of the again-roofless San Juan chapel while a coffin lid braces the frame of the north window. A remnant of the fallen stone cross from the top of the espadaña remains lodged where it fell, upper right. Still visible around the inside doorway are original frescoes painted to resemble colored stone blocks.

a series of hurricanes took off the roof of San Juan's chapel, which became derelict once more. The Catholic Church still sought to maintain its ownership at San Juan, although Bishop John C. Neraz in 1893 lost a legal fight to recover some of the former mission property.

The first private attempt to restore the San Juan chapel was made in the fall of 1902, when pioneer San Antonio preservationist Adina De Zavala obtained a five-year lease on the chapel on behalf of San Antonio's chapter of the Daughters of the Republic of Texas.

As in the case of leases on former mission churches between the Landmarks Club of California and Catholic dioceses there, the Daughters could restore San Juan, hire a custodian, charge admis-

A general store served Mission San Juan area residents at nearby Berg's Mill.

sion and keep the fees as long as the church could still be used for worship services. At that point, however, Miss De Zavala was distracted by conflict over saving the Alamo convento, and her plan for San Juan did not materialize.

Following the death of Father Bouchu in 1907, the San Juan' chapel was included with Espada's in repairs directed by architect Leo M. J. Dielmann. Once repairs were completed in 1909, services were once again held in the chapel, under the charge of the Claretian order.

Two decades later the San Antonio Conservation Society, having undertaken major restoration at San José, laid plans to purchase land around San Juan's plaza. But the society's preservation plans at San Juan were thwarted by the Depression, which, on the other hand, produced federally funded workers to make repairs. In 1934 they reroofed the chapel. Unfinished walls of the church across the plaza were partly rebuilt on the old foundations, revealed by excavations.

To provide quarters for Franciscans returning to San Juan, and to attract visitors expected for the upcoming HemisFair '68, in 1967 the Catholic archdiocese rebuilt the priests' quarters on the western edge of the plaza, preceded by an extensive archeological excavation directed by Mardith Schuetz. The project was supervised by Father Balthasar Janacek, later the archdiocesan liason for the missions with the city, state and National Park Service.

A lithograph of ruins of the Mission San Juan Capistrano compound, at top, was reproduced from a circa 1856 painting by Hermann Lungkwitz. With completion in 1909 of the chapel's restoration, below, a stone cross was back atop the espadaña, the center door was reopened and a picket fence separated the chapel from the public road that cut across the old mission compound.

With the mission under the wing of the National Park Service, on October 12, 1992, precisely 500 years after the arrival of Christopher Columbus and the beginning of Spanish influence in the New World, a crowd of 200 gathered near Mission San Juan to watch Secretary of the Interior Manuel Lujan pull a wooden lever to send water from the river back into the ancient San Juan acequia, dry since its dam washed out more than two decades before.

This time water was to irrigate a future Spanish colonial demonstration farm, to have workers in period costumes and oxen tilling the types of crops once raised by San Juan's mission Indians.

To enhance Mission San Juan in time for visitors to
HemisFair '68 and also to provide quarters for Franciscan
priests returning to serve the mission parish, the Archdiocese of San Antonio in 1967 began archeological
excavations and reconstruction of buildings north of the
chapel. At right, Floyd Tristan displays candleholders,
square nails, broken pottery and unidentified
bones discovered during the work.

Reconstructed buildings on the west side of San Juan's mission plaza house parish priests who conduct services in the restored mission church, its altar, left, bearing 18th century statues authentic to the mission's era.

7. Mission San Francisco de la Espada

A familiar symbol of Mission Espada is its chapel's unusual doorway (*facing page*). Although many believe the broken line of its outer arc is due to the stones having been improperly placed, its style generally has been considered Moorish. But the style may be older. Franciscan architects could have been influenced by the Visigothic style church of San Juan Bautista (*above, as photographed by Eugene George*), built in 661 AD in the village of Baños de Cerrato in northern Spain, which has similarities to Espada's chapel.

Furthest south of San Antonio's five missions is San Francisco de la Espada, the fourth incarnation of the first mission established in Spanish Texas.

The mission was first established on May 24, 1690 as Mission San Francisco de los Tejas by the Querétaran Franciscan missionary Damian Massanet. Located near present-day Nacogdoches in East Texas, the mission was abandoned three years later. It was reborn ten miles away in 1716 as Mission Nuestro Padre San Francisco de los Tejas.

Three years after that the mission was abandoned again, this time due to hostility from the French. It was reestablished in 1721 on the Neches River as Mission San Francisco de los Neches to serve the Neche Indians, a Caddoan tribe.

Eight years later the mission's movable assets joined those of its two sister East Texas Querétaran missions on the trek westward to the Colorado River and, finally, to San Antonio. It was reestablished on March 5, 1731 on its present site on the west bank of the San Antonio River to serve at first the Pacao, Borrado and Mariquita tribes of Coahuiltecans. This time, to San Francisco was appended the apparent surname de la Espada—"of the sword"—of since-forgotten origin.

Within its first six years, Mission San Francisco de la Espada suffered Apache raids that took its horses, then an epidemic of smallpox and measles followed by a desertion of its entire population of 230 Indians.

Discipline had begun to break down early in 1737, when one Indian was promised punishment for violating mission rules. Other Indians, however, threatened the missionary with violence if the punishment occurred, and the perpetrator was left undisciplined. Disenchanted, Espada's Tecame Indians, who had previously abandoned Mission San José, departed.

When Espada's remaining Indians saw that the captain of the San Antonio presidio refused to send soldiers to pursue the Tecames, despite the need for them to help harvest crops, they also left. Then the presidio was assigned a new captain. After repeated messengers failed to lure many Indians back, the new captain and nine soldiers went out in pursuit. After 21 days of searching they returned with nearly half of the defectors.

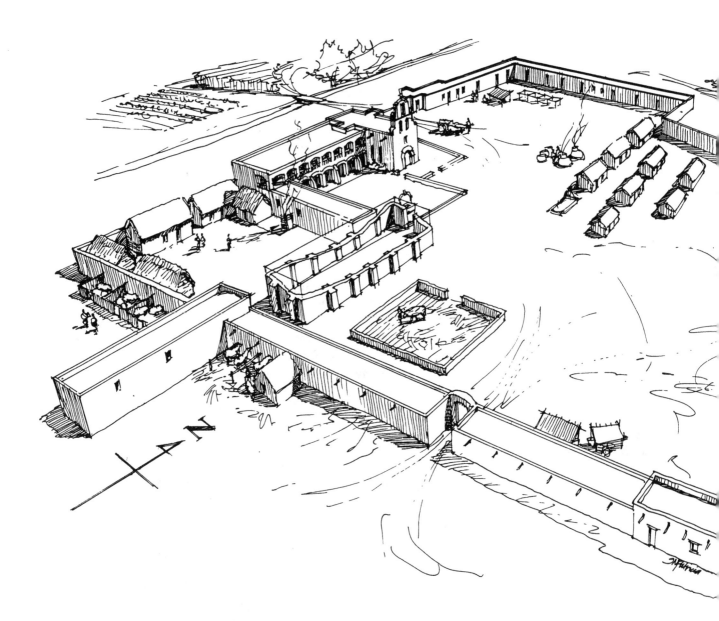

About 1780, a thatch-roofed blacksmith shop backs onto the two-story convento adjoining Mission Espada's chapel. Surrounding its courtyard are four similar buildings, used for storing lumber and wool, and the walls of the mission church, torn down after being found structurally unsound and in danger of collapse. A fenced threshing area is to its right. The long building extending past the wall at lower left is the granary. Mission indians lived in housing in the plaza and in quarters around the wall at center top. Outside the compound at left runs the mission acequia—still in use—while, at right, are kilns for baking brick. Spanish troops quartered in the compound in the early nineteenth century added a round bastion, which survives, in the perimeter wall at lower right.

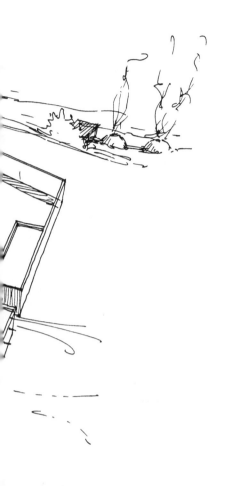

Soon the Epidemic of 1739 and more runaways cut Espada's Indian population from 120 to 50. But with new recruits the number was back at 120 by the end of 1740 and up five years later to 204. Of those, 180 were already baptized. Since the mission moved to San Antonio, 393 Indians had been baptized there, and Christian burials were given to 213.

To help missionaries make rituals understandable to the Indians, Father Bartholomé García, assistant to Father Acisclos Valverde, prepared in the general Coahuiltecan language a book published in Mexico in 1760 under the title *Manual para Administrar los Santos Sacramentos*. It is termed the first textbook of Texas.

By 1745 Espada's convento was completed. By 1756 so was the temporary chapel, with a two-tiered espadaña above its entrance. Above the altar, which doubled as a four-drawer walnut chest containing vestments, was a three-foot statue of the mission's patron saint, St. Francis. Three-foot-square paintings of San Bernardino and St. John of Capistrano were hung on either side. In addition to silver communion pieces, five sets of multi-colored vestments and a baptismal font, the chapel's accoutrements included two rugs.

Later the chapel got benches, two confessional booths and a gilded tabernacle for the main altar, while a second altar honored Our Lady of the Rosary. A statue of Our Lady of Sorrows on a portable stand was carried in processions.

A large church, intended as the final one, was begun by 1762 and completed with rock from a new quarry near Espada. But the new church was found to be structurally unsound and by 1777 was torn down before it could collapse. Services went back to the old chapel, which was to have become the sacristy for the larger church.

Turreted stone walls protected the isolated headquarters of Mission Espada's Rancho de las Cabras—"Ranch of the Goats"—from hostile Indians tempted by the ranch's herds of livestock. The fortifications enclosed a stone chapel, living quarters, corral and a well. The site is now owned by the National Park Service.

RANDALL L. HOHLAUS, AIA

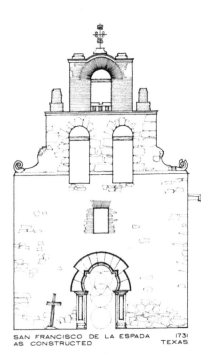

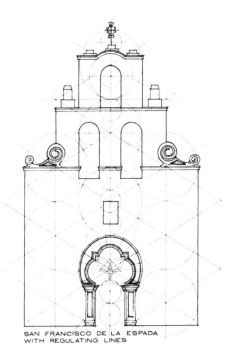

SAN FRANCISCO DE LA ESPADA   1731
AS CONSTRUCTED   TEXAS

SAN FRANCISCO DE LA ESPADA
WITH REGULATING LINES

SAN FRANCISCO DE LA ESPADA
AS PROPOSED (CONJECTURAL)

Why the stones of the irregularly arched doorway of Espada's chapel were placed as they were has long been a matter of speculation. One solution to the mystery is suggested by architectural historian Eugene George.

The same stones can be rearranged to form a smooth outer arc. The doorway would then conform neatly to the architectural principles which George determined were used in the design of the rest of the facade. Those include a pattern of regulating lines of circles—symbolizing, to church architects, divine perfection—and diagonally oriented squares, symbolic of earthly existence.

How did the Espada doorway turn out as it did? Its stones, he believes, could have been precut on the site under the direction of a master stonemason known to have been staying at Espada but who may have left to supervise a project elsewhere before the Espada project was completed.

Workmen left behind, having never seen such a pattern, may not have comprehended instructions for assembling the doorway's stones, and put them together as best they could.

The two-story stone convento facing Espada's mission plaza included workrooms housing three looms and spinning wheels. Nearby were a large stone granary and Indian houses of brush and mud, later replaced with three rows of stone houses. Other quarters lined the inside of nearby perimeter walls. Construction was aided with brick fired in the mission's kilns beyond the northern wall. For protection, 16 firearms were issued and turrets on perimeter walls got swivel guns.

The wonder of the adjoining farmland was a double-arched stone aqueduct across Piedras Creek that carried the acequia's waters from the wing-shaped diversion dam two miles north and to the mission fields. It is the oldest stone aqueduct still in operation in the United States. Espada's farmland at this time was producing 1,600 bushels of corn each year, plus beans, melons, pumpkins and cotton.

Thirty miles to the south, Espada's ranch—Rancho de las Cabras, "Ranch of the Goats"—supported 1,150 head of cattle, 740 sheep, 90 goats, 81 horses and 16 yoke of oxen. As the ranch thrived, the number of cattle increased to 1,262 and sheep to 4,000. Vaqueros had their own stone chapel and quarters near corrals, all surrounded by gated stone walls with two fortified turrets.

By 1794, Mission San Francisco de la Espada's Indian population had dropped to 45, in 15 families. On July 11 of that year Manuel Múñoz, the Spanish governor of Texas, rode from San Antonio to Espada to personally announce the start of secularization of the four southern missions.

The next day, Pedro Huizar began surveying Espada's mission lands for division among its 15 families. Father Pedro Noreña, at Espada since 1778, remained to serve both Espada and Mission San Juan Capistrano.

By the early 1880s there was little left of Espada's chapel but its crumbling facade. The mission's Spanish aqueduct, however, remained intact, carrying the acequia's waters over Piedras Creek and offering a secluded spot for washing clothes and bathing.

Father Francis Bouchu, an immigrant French lay priest, moved from Mission San Juan to Espada in 1885 and began reconstructing the main part of the old convento, above center, as his residence. He opened a community store in another part, far left. Two years later Father Bouchu, shown at right about 1900, finished rebuilding the mission chapel, where he held services until his death in 1907 at the age of 78.

TOP: DRT LIBRARY AT THE ALAMO; BELOW: CATHOLIC ARCHIVES, AUSTIN, TEXAS

A rare ice storm about 1903 occasioned the top photo of the Espada Store, by then being run by a local resident, housed in part of the old mission convento. About the same time the family above was being photographed inside the rebuilt mission chapel, an adobe house on the northern edge of the compound was being braced and restored.

Though the decline of Espada's Indian population paralleled that at the other missions, the influx of Spanish settlers to the Espada neighborhood exceeded the rate at the others. By 1815 there were nearly three times as many Spaniards at Espada as Indians—72 Spaniards and 27 Indians, forming the nucleus of a community that survives to this day.

After Mission Espada was closed in 1824 and its church was turned over to San Antonio's parish church of San Fernando, the Espada community shared the region's political instability. A Comanche raid in the spring of 1826 wiped out the livestock, damaged crops and wounded several men, causing a company of Mexican troops to be sent to Espada from Coahuila to protect the area. To the mission's south wall the soldiers added a round stone bastion, which remains.

Mexican soldiers fled on October 22, 1835, as 100 American colonists led by James Bowie and James W. Fannin Jr. moved to-

TOP AND BELOW RIGHT: THE INSTITUTE OF TEXAN CULTURES, COURTESY MRS. MARY PERSYN; BELOW LEFT: CATHOLIC ARCHIVES, AUSTIN, TEXAS

Mission Espada   93

San Antonio's skyline some eight miles away barely appears near the center horizon in this aerial view looking northwest above Mission Espada about 1935. As was the case with San Antonio's other missions, most of the outer walls had been scavanged for building materials and roadways were cut through the former plaza. Espada's bastion and adjoining perimeter building are off picture at lower right.

ward the old mission. Three days later the Texans successfully defended themselves within its walls from an attack by a Mexican force twice as large.

By midcentury, Mission Espada lay in ruins. Soon only the chapel's facade remained. The granary stood, as did walls on two sides of the square, but many other buildings had been destroyed by fire. Nevertheless, the irrigated fields kept families living within the old mission compound and in scattered homes nearby.

To the rescue came Father Francis Bouchu, the French-born priest who had lived across the river at the old San Juan mission and restored its chapel. In 1885 he moved to Espada.

The versatile Francis Bouchu was, in the words of the contemporary writer William Corner, "priest, lawyer, bricklayer, stone mason, photographer, historian, printer." And storekeeper as well. At Espada he set about rebuilding the remains of the convento into his residence—with a French-style hip roof—and remodeling one end of the convento as a general store, which he at first operated himself. Using profits from the store and from personal real estate transactions, Father Bouchu purchased adjoining former mission tracts from private hands.

Boys sat on one side and girls on the other in Sister Superior Alma's classroom in one of Espada's old mission buildings by the bastion in 1941. At right, Sister Alma doubles as an arm-banded air raid warden with Sister Marie de San José during World War II. Barely a mile and a half to Espada's north and west were two airfields—Brooks, an Army Air Corps pilot training center, and Stinson, then San Antonio's municipal airport.

In 1887 Father Bouchu completed rebuilding the Espada chapel as his parish church, complete with choir loft and pews. He regilded three surviving statues, including the one of St. Francis, and placed them on the new altar.

Just as, a century before, Espada's Father Bartolomé García prepared a translation of religious services in their native language for his Coahuiltecan-speaking communicants, so did Father Bouchu produce a catechism in Spanish for his Spanish-speaking communicants. The work went into its fourth edition in 1897 after being adopted for use throughout the diocese and was printed by Father Bouchu on his own press.

Father Bouchu's path crossed that of pioneer San Antonio preservationist Adina De Zavala, who visited him at Espada with a friend in the summer of 1903. He offered to share his noon-day meal of fried onions, cream cheese and bread, but the ladies declined.

Father Bouchu died in 1907 at the age of 78. Two years later, services at Espada were transferred to the newly repaired chapel at San Juan. The Espada chapel reopened in 1911 with a new roof, new ceiling, new doors and windows and a brick floor.

Sisters of Charity of the Incarnate Word in 1915 opened a school, which in the course of its 52 years of existence incorporated a classroom formed by the walls of the bastion built by the Mexican Army. The multicultural mix of the agrarian region was reflected by the ethnic origins of the school's early students—Spanish, Mexican, Italian, Belgian, German, Anglo.

Federally funded workers stabilized ruins at Espada in the early 1930s. In 1937 the San Antonio Conservation Society purchased the aqueduct and six and a half surrounding acres. In a yearlong restoration effort begun in 1955 by Archbishop Robert E. Lucey, workers guided by architect Harvey P. Smith braced and

The first two rows of benches were reserved for girls and the benches behind them for women in 1915, four years after Espada's chapel reopened following an extensive renovation. A statue of St. Francis, the mission's patron saint, remained above the altar.

reconstructed portions of the old walls and rerouted the public road that had crossed the plaza. Into the partially rebuilt convento came, in 1967, the returning Franciscans.

Another round of major restorations conducted by the National Park Service in 1984 turned up in the building destined to become Espada's visitors center a floor of heavy flagstones, part of the grain threshing floor which once extended into the mission plaza. Twenty-five miles south, near Floresville, the State of Texas carried out excavations on the 100 acres it owned of Espada's Rancho de las Cabras, revealing locations of the original headquarters buildings. The state donated its property to the National Park Service in 1995.

In early 1998, wiring under Mission Espada's chapel roof short-circuited, starting a fire—quickly extinguished—that damaged the roof and interior and handed the archdiocese the problem of restoration.

Since the original interior had crumbled in the mid-nineteenth century and no description survived, architects decided to reconstruct the type of wooden roof designed by Harvey Smith in 1961, using, however, cypress beams rather than the previous railroad ties as supports. Also, the small attic would be better reconfigured for the air conditioning units invaluable during hot summer days—a signal improvement from times of yore, when five Spanish missions flourished at San Antonio.

Archbishop Robert E. Lucey holds the drawings as he inspects work on Espada's south gate, as a major Catholic Archdiocesan restoration project gets under way in 1955. At his left stands architect Harvey P. Smith, who guided the major work at Mission San José two decades before. At his right is contractor Louis Guido. The gateway is recessed in the compound's south wall near far left of the photo at right, which shows the bastion added by Spanish soldiers in the early 1800s.

Espada's chapel was intended to become the sacristy for the mission church—its restored foundations in the foreground—but reverted to use for services when the newly-built church was found to be structurally unsound and was torn down about 1777. At the left of the chapel is the partly-restored convento, with changes made by Father Francis Bouchu a century ago since removed.

The restored cloisters of Mission Espada's convento front the quarters
of priests assigned to the present-day Espada parish.

Chronology

1537— Pope Paul III decrees "Indians are truly men capable of understanding the Catholic faith," enabling missionary efforts in the New World.

1573— Missionary work begins in Florida.

1598— Franciscans begin missions in New Mexico.

1690— Franciscans found two missions in East Texas.

1691— Expedition to East Texas missions discovers headwaters, names San Antonio River.

1693— East Texas missions closed.

1716— East Texas missions reestablished.

1718— Founding of Mission San Antonio de Valero and a presidio begin the city of San Antonio.

1720— Mission San José founded.

1722— Mission San Francisco Xavier de Nájera founded.

1724— Mission San Antonio de Valero moves to its present site.

1726— Mission San Francisco Xavier de Nájera merges with Mission San Antonio de Valero.

1731— Three East Texas missions reestablished at San Antonio as Concepción, San Juan, Espada.

1739— Epidemic of smallpox and measles, region's worst, decimates mission Indian populace.

1740— Mission San José moves to its present site.

1745— Present Mission Espada chapel in use.

1755— Mission Concepción church dedicated.

1756— Mission San Antonio de Valero church under way; present San Juan chapel in use.

1768— Cornerstone laid for San José church.

1769— Franciscans begin missions in California.

1771— San Juan missionary leads expedition to gather new converts in futile effort to reverse mission Indian population decline.

1782— Mission San José church completed.

1793— Mission San Antonio de Valero closed.

1794— Secularization begins at remaining missions.

1803— Spanish cavalry unit from Alamo de Parras moves into former San Antonio de Valero.

1824— Last four San Antonio missions closed.

1835— Texans defeat Mexican army near Mission Concepción, defend themselves at Espada.

1836— Texans annihilated at former San Antonio de Valero mission.

1841— Republic of Texas reaffirms Catholic Church ownership of former Spanish mission churches.

1845— U.S. Army begins 22 years of use of Mission San Antonio de Valero/Alamo as supply depot.

1855— Catholic Church resumes use of Mission Concepción church.

1859— Catholic Church resumes use of San José church as Benedictines move in.

1874— San José's church dome and roof collapse.

1877— Father Bouchu restores San Juan chapel.

1883— State makes first purchase of San Antonio de Valero/Alamo property for its battle memories.

1887— Father Bouchu rebuilds Espada chapel.

1902— Daughters of the Republic of Texas begin first private restoration effort at San José.

1911— Catholic church expands its restoration program at mission churches.

1928— San José church tower collapses.

1929— San Antonio Conservation Society begins purchasing land to preserve San José mission compound; first community effort begins for roadway linking all missions.

1931— Franciscans return to San José.

1933— Conservation Society opens restored San José mission granary.

1936— Federal relief workers complete rebuilt San José mission plaza and mill.

1937— Catholic Church dedicates restored San José church; Conservation Society buys Espada aqueduct.

1941— San José Mission State Park created.

1955— Major repairs at Mission Espada.

1967— First bill to create a missions national park introduced in Congress; major restoration at Mission San Juan.

1978— San Antonio Missions National Historical Park created.

1983— Missions National Historical Park opens.

1988— International team restores frescoes at Mission Concepción.

1996— Park visitors center is completed at San José.

1998— Mission bicycle and hiking trails, renewed Mission Road programs begin.

Selected Bibliography

Almaráz, Felix D. Jr. *The San Antonio Missions and Their System of Land Tenure.* Austin: University of Texas Press, 1989.

Chipman, Donald E. *Spanish Texas, 1519–1821.* Austin: University of Texas Press, 1992.

Corner, William. *San Antonio de Bexar: A Guide and History.* San Antonio: Bainbridge & Coiner, 1890, reprinted 1977 by Mary Ann Noonan-Guerra.

Fisher, Lewis F. *Saving San Antonio: The Precarious Preservation of a Heritage.* Lubbock: Texas Tech University Press, 1996.

Foster, Nancy Haston. *Texas Missions.* Houston: Gulf Publishing, 1995.

Fox, Daniel E. *Traces of Texas History: Archeological Evidence of the Past 450 Years.* San Antonio: Corona Publishing Co., 1983.

Habig, Marion A., O.F.M. *The Alamo Chain of Missions.* Chicago: Franciscan Herald Press, 1968, reprinted 1997 by Pioneer Enterprises.

Henry, Jay C. *Architecture in Texas, 1895–1945.* Austin: University of Texas Press, 1993.

Jackson, Jack. *Los Mesteños: Spanish Ranching in Texas 1721–1821.* College Station: Texas A&M University Press, 1986.

James and Juarez, Architects, and others. *San Antonio Missions: Cultural Landscape Report.* Vol. 1. Santa Fe: National Park Service, 1996.

Jordan, Terry G. *North American Cattle-Ranching Frontiers.* Albuquerque: University of New Mexico Press, 1993.

Poyo, Gerald E., and Gilberto M. Hinojosa. *Tejano Origins in Eighteenth-Century San Antonio.* Austin: University of Texas Press, 1991.

Simons, Helen, and Cathryn A. Hoyt. *Hispanic Texas: A Historical Guide.* Austin: University of Texas Press, 1992.

de la Teja, Jesús F. *San Antonio de Bexar: A Community on New Spain's Northern Frontier.* Albuquerque: University of New Mexico Press, 1995.

Thurber, Marlys Bush. "Building the Missions of San Antonio" in *Texas Architect,* May–June 1986, pp. 54–58.

_____, and others. *Of Various Magnificence: The Architectural History of the San Antonio Missions in the Colonial Period and the Nineteenth Century.* 2 vols. Santa Fe: National Park Service, 1993.

Torres, Luis. *San Antonio Missions.* Tucson: Southwest Parks and Monuments Assoc., 1993.

_____. *Voices from the San Antonio Missions.* Lubbock: Texas Tech University Press, 1997.

Tyler, Ron, ed. *The New Handbook of Texas.* 6 vols. Austin: The Texas State Historical Association, 1996.

Weber, David J. *The Spanish Frontier in North America.* New Haven and London: Yale University Press, 1992.

Weddle, Robert S. *San Juan Bautista, Gateway to Spanish Texas.* Austin: University of Texas Press, 1968.

Acknowledgments

Special thanks for assistance go, at San Antonio Missions National Historical Park, to Park Historian Dr. Rosalind Rock for reviewing the manuscript and to Cherry Payne, Santiago Escobedo and Superintendent Stephen Whitesell; at the University of Texas Institute of Texan Cultures at San Antonio to Photo Archivist Tom Shelton and Chris Floerke; to Martha Utterback and staff at the Daughters of the Republic of Texas Library at the Alamo; Rebecca Hufstuttler at the Witte Museum; Nelle Lee Weincek at the San Antonio Conservation Society Library; Brother Edward Loch at the Catholic Chancery; Sheila Jordan at the National Park Service's Harpers Ferry Center; architects Eugene George and Carolyn Peterson; and to my ever-supportive family. — *Lewis F. Fisher*

Index

Lewis F. Fisher's books
include *Brackenridge: San
Antonio's Acclaimed Urban
Park, American Venice: The
Epic Story of San Antonio's
River, Saving San Antonio:
The Preservation of a Heri-
tage, Maverick: The American
Name That Became a Leg-
end,* and *Chili Queens, Hay
Wagons, and Fandangos: The
Spanish Plazas in Frontier
San Antonio.* He lives in
San Antonio, Texas.